© Copyright 1986 by:

HORST ZIETHEN VERLAG
D-5000 Köln 50 / Germany
Unter Buschweg 17
☎ (0 22 36) 6 10 28

1. impression / 1. Auflage / première édition

printed by / Druck / imprimé par

OFFSET-FARBDRUCK HORST ZIETHEN
D-5000 Köln 50 / Germany

ISBN 3-921268-35-4

author / Autor / auteur
HANS-OTTO MEISSNER

translated by / Übersetzung / traduction:
Gwendolen Freundel (english)
France Varry (français)

photographs / Fotografie / photographies
KARL KINNE · Exclusivphotographie

additional photographs / Zusatzaufnahmen / autres photographies
Horst Niesters · Gamephotographer: 49, 71, 77, 106, 127
Silvestris Fotoservice: 51, 76 rechts, 135
Mauritius: 122, 141 · Hans-Otto Meissner: 78, 102 · The Image Bank: 107
Hanns-Josef Kaiser: map / Landkarte / carte géographique

Hans-Otto Meissner
Photographs by Karl Kinne

english text page 5

THE WONDERS OF
CALIFORNIA
THROUGH THE AMERICAN SOUTHWEST

deutscher Text Seite 14

WUNDERBARES
KALIFORNIEN
DURCH DEN SÜDWESTEN DER USA

Texte en français page 23

LA CALIFORNIE
A TRAVERS LE SUD-OUEST
DES ETATS-UNIS

Horst Ziethen Verlag

The Wonders of California

To talk of California when one is in America is to mean far more than just the state of that name. California is really a term for a region that has no present-day boundaries, for it encompasses roughly the area which was discovered, explored or in any way affected by the Spaniards and which, at least on paper, all belonged to Mexico until 1848.

These lands bordering on California share to a great extent its climate, geology and landscape, and it seems to me a logical step to include them in our book. Visitors to the area will certainly agree with me that we should not restrict ourselves to the rigid confines dictated by the map-makers.

California has everything to offer that anyone could ever wish for on this earth. It has a temperate climate, good soil and an average of two hundred and fifty days sunshine a year; there are sandy bathing beaches set in a coastline of breathtaking beauty, snow-covered mountains, lush forests and valleys of fabulous splendour. Vast, windswept plateaus can suddenly blossom into a sea of flowers; there are thorny wastes, cactus forests, oases with palms and bubbling springs, entrancing lakes of every shape and colour, some high in mountains whose summits are never free from snow – the wonders of California have no end.

California is the third largest state of the USA and extends nearly eight hundred miles along the Pacific coast, that is, through ten degrees of latitude; in breadth it ranges from one hundred and forty to more than six hundred miles. The total area is a vast 160,000 square miles, in comparison with the 96,000 square miles of the Federal Republic of Germany, although its population is only 22 million compared with Germany's 60 million. Nevertheless, California's population is steadily increasing, owing to an influx of people from other states of the USA and to (often illegal) immigrants from Mexico.

California is the land of superlatives. It possesses the highest mountain in the 48 contiguous states, Mount Whitney, 14,494 feet high, and the lowest point in America, indeed in the western hemisphere, Badswater in Death Valley, 282 feet below sea level. Death Valley, about three thousand square miles of hot, dry, dusty land, is one of the designated National Monuments or National Parks. The term "park" is apt to be misleading to foreigners, for it refers in this case not to cultivated parkland but to just the opposite, an area to be left as far as possible in its original state.

California presents a challenge to anyone hoping to see all the superlatives it has to offer; what is more, there are so many seemingly irreconcilable opposites. This go-ahead state has the largest, tallest and oldest trees in the world, for example. In Methuselah Park on the border with Nevada stand dozens of windswept bristlecone pines that were already in existence when the Pharaoh Cheops began building his pyramid.

There are active volcanoes in California which occasionally erupt and destroy huge areas, as Mount St. Helens did recently in Washington state. Earthquakes are no rarity either; San Francisco was destroyed by a conflagration in the wake of an earthquake at the beginning of the century.

Practically everything flourishes in California. Tropical fruits are an example; introduced by the Spanish missionaries, they thrive here. And the right soil and climate for all sorts of different fruits are to be found, not only in one but in several areas of this land of milk and honey. Whatever the pioneers brought from Europe or from their various corners of the earth, it grew and multiplied with ease, and in the list we can include sheep, cattle, goats, horses, donkeys and all kinds of poultry, with the exception of turkeys, an export from Central America to Europe.

There are rich reserves of gold, silver, copper and oil, not to speak of other desirable raw materials, whose supplies have by no means been exhausted. If we turn to transport, there is an adequate network of good roads for the sightseer, four or five lane highways whose speed limit is nevertheless no more than fifty-five m.p.h.

The most beautiful road in California, said to be the most fantastic in the world, is the State Highway No. 1, better known as the BIG SUR. Its most impressive section is undoubtedly the incomparable scenic route along the coast between Monterey and Morro Bay, where the road goes careering up and down hill and around headlands, forcing the driver to enjoy the luxury of driving slowly. The greatest care must be taken here on all sides, but every bend in the road reveals a view of astounding beauty, a kaleidoscope of cliffs and colours, surging breakers, gently retreating waves, floating fields of sea-grass, islands that tower out of the ocean like church steeples and deeply-cut valleys reminiscent of Norwegian fjords. The whole area of the BIG SUR is more deserted than any other part of California. It always has been, since the day in 1770 when a Franciscan friar, Father Junipero Serra, founded his Carmel mission on St Lucia Bay among a few hundred nomads who lived in the most primitive fashion imaginable.

The mountains around the BIG SUR are the home of the high chapparal, a wilderness of thorn bushes where neither sheep nor cows can exist, and certainly no pastures, fields or vegetable plots will survive. For a long time no settlers ventured here, but the first, a German named Pfeifer, managed to eke out an existence, and subsequently his numerous descendants began to tap the resources of the area. Many settlements, mountains and rivers are called after the Pfeifer family. It remained to William Randolph Hearst in later years to create the fabulous collection of palaces, museums and parks known as SAN SIMEON, on which the press baron and master of Hollywood is supposed to have spent over one thousand million dollars.

The many "VISTAPOINTS" along this road are a great attraction for tourists, providing a parking place and the chance to enjoy a panoramic view. Armed with patience and a good pair of field-glasses, one can spot sea-lions, seals and, with luck, walruses on the beaches, while out to sea there are sperm whales, grey whales and even the occasional blue whale, the largest animal in the world. Another unforgettable sight is that of the sea otters, which were long subject to such merciless slaughter on account of their valuable fur that these magnificent and harmless creatures were assumed to have died out at the end of the last century. Miraculously, some reappeared in 1937 and, as a strictly protected animal, have now managed to increase their numbers to over one hundred thousand.

We can trace the same sort of phenomenal development in the immigrants, who came mainly from the eastern states and from Europe. Outwardly, most Californians are tall, healthy, cheerful and active. They are usually self-confident and optimistic, although they do not take kindly to criticism of their country and their people, for California, the thirty-first and most populous state, prides itself on being the land of the superlative, no less than the epitome of "the land of the free and the home of the brave".

In addition to the four great National Parks in California, all of them well-maintained, there are another eighteen nature reserves enjoying special legal protection. For those of us who come from overpopulated and built-up Europe, it is quite extraordinary to witness the successful efforts the Californians have made to protect their environment.

It all began with the Spaniards, albeit very few, who arrived from Mexico and made their way up to the north-west. The architecture, the animals and the horticulture that they brought with them are still dominating factors in the life of the state. Some present-day highways run along the same routes as once did the missionaries' mule tracks, and cities with millions of inhabitants were founded on the sites of mission buildings and therefore still bear the names of Roman Catholic saints.

The History of the American Southwest

California was discovered and its southern limits explored in about the year 1535, by no less a person than HERNANDO CORTEZ, conqueror and subsequent viceroy of Mexico. It was not, however, the area corresponding to the present state, but the relatively narrow peninsula known as Baja California, roughly six hundred miles long and today a part of Mexico. This early attempt to settle in such a remote region was doomed to failure, and further exploration was left to the buccaneers, who navigated the coast and eventually reached Canada, perhaps even Alaska. The first European to land in what we now understand as California was probably HERNANDO DE ALARCON in about 1540, but the Spaniards did not venture anywhere inland at that time, for the Spanish empire was already unwieldy and the reserves of the mother country did not stretch to the occupation of such territory. Only the sheltered MONTEREY BAY held any real importance, being a halting-place for the trading fleet that cruised twice a year between ACAPULCO harbour, on the west coast of Mexico, and MANILA, the capital of the Spanish Philippines.

At that time one spoke of LAS CALIFORNIAS, in the plural, and this actually referred to an enormous area comprising the coastline and hinterland from Baja California in the south up to the far north, as far as Spanish ships had ever sailed. In Spanish eyes these territories were all in the possession of the Spanish crown.

It was not until the years around 1700 that the first deliberate exploration and settlement of California began. The first mission was erected in LA PAZ at the southern tip of Lower California in about 1691 and the last, SAN SOLANO, north of San Francisco Bay, in 1822. That was a chain of thirty-one missions extending over two thousand miles as the crow flies. The chain included the Baja California missions and for those times it was an amazing and enormous feat. Twenty-one of the missions were in present-day California and they were linked by a track that, despite its name, – El Camino Real, the King's Highway – was of course only frequented by rumbling ox-carts, horses, mules, and most commonly, people on foot bearing heavy burdens.

Most of the missions in Baja California have fallen into ruin in the last few decades and only parts of the Camino Real are still to be seen. I tried in vain to walk along it for a few miles. In the state of California, on the other hand, all the missions still stand or have been rebuilt, not exactly according to the original, but nevertheless so competently that they are imbued with the feeling of their original atmosphere. It is possible to see some of the original furnishings, the guest rooms reserved for officers and civil servants, and altars in the churches and chapels in which the founder of the first mission, Father Junipero Serra, once preached. Visitors can see quite clearly from the layout of the buildings how the missions were organised and which tasks the individual stations set themselves. They not only endeavoured to administer Christian baptism to the heathen Indians to save their souls from damnation, but also undertook to teach them a degree of self-sufficiency and to improve their social organisation. The natives of California were hardly able to feed themselves or to defend themselves adequately against enemies, animal or human; their culture certainly bears no comparison with that of the Mayas and Aztecs, the Mesa Indians and the Pueblos.

Six, seven or eight nomadic tribes roamed the area at this time, all with different customs and languages. Contemporary reports describe them as extremely timid, shy and subsequently obedient; they approached the friars voluntarily, trusting that the missions would feed, shelter and protect them. Judging by the results of the tasks they were given and by the rapidity with which they learned new skills, they showed very varying levels in intelligence and in willingness to learn. Some succeeded in mastering the art of the blacksmith, the potter and the weaver; others managed to learn reading, writing and arithmetic. There were also tribes and groups of natives who simply defied all attempts at conversion. It was not unknown for them to attack the missions and beat the defenceless Franciscans to death. For this reason, each station was meant to house a "PRESIDIO", that is, a bodyguard consisting of an officer in charge of ten or twelve Spanish soldiers. This situation unfortunately led to frequent difficulties between the friars and the military. The soldiers, usually unruly young men, chased the girls, got drunk on the wine that had been especially grown for the Mass, and apart from that gave a bad example to the baptised Indian children. The devout Franciscans therefore insisted that the Presidios should be quartered some miles away from the mission and its flock. Consequently, the soldiers invariably arrived too late when the savage Indios launched an attack. In the end, the Franciscans succeeded in making good workers out of these children of nature. A number of the baptised Indians developed true artistic capabilities, and in many missions it is still possible to admire Indian paintings and carvings, each with its own distinctive style. The stations were self-sufficient, producing all the necessities of life in and around the mission buildings. It gradually became feasible to export products like soap and tanned leather, wax candles and bone meal, to Mexico and even back to the Spanish homeland. Standing in one of the reconstructed missions, one feels a sense of wonder, not to say amazement, at the number of workshops and the amount of agricultural instruments, all demonstrating how efficient the organisation was. I might add that the holy fathers did not put all their trust in the morals of their flock, for at sundown all the young women and married women whose husbands were not present were locked up for the night.

In the summer of 1769, SAN DIEGO, situated near the Mexican border, became the first Franciscan mission to be founded in what we now know as California. It was the tireless Father Junipero Serra who accompanied, or rather led, Captain Gaspar de Portola here overland from Mexico. The Franciscan had been the first to undertake incredibly long and difficult journeys on foot through this totally unexplored terrain to find possible future routes. In the footsteps of the missionaries and soldiers followed two hundred and twenty settlers, including children, of Spanish descent. They took with them what animals they could, along with the necessary seeds and indispensable agricultural implements. Since it was reckoned that the losses would be high, or that the whole party would never be seen again, three ships carrying groups of settlers, soldiers and missionaries were dispatched along the sea route. In fact, two thirds of the overland expedition reached their goal and two of the three ships arrived in San Diego Bay, though hunger, thirst and disease had depleted the number of passengers and crew by more than half.

Hardly had the station been established in the most primitive fashion before the journey was continued up into the unknown north, soldiers and settlers trailing along behind their leader, Father Junipero Serra, the creaking ox-carts trundling after. At roughly the same time, the two cumbersome ships were struggling to reach a pre-arranged destination. Every such advance was accompanied by heavy losses, but that was seen as inevitable, and a few dozen souls always managed to battle through. Thus were founded such missions as CARLOS BORROMEO DE CARMELO and SAN ANTONIO DE PADUA, LUIS OBISPO and SAN JUAN CAPSTRANO, SANTA CLARA and SANTA BARBARA. In September 1771 SAN GABRIEL ARCANGEL was set up. Only with the aid of a detailed city plan of Los Angeles is it possible to find it, the old, beautifully restored Franciscan mission, tucked away amidst the maze of houses that make up this city of seven million people. The Captain and Father Serra arranged for the colony of settlers to be housed with their families and animals several miles from San Gabriel, where the wicked Presidio could not disturb the conversion work of the friars. This settlement is also still in existence, the nucleus of a city in parts over sixty miles wide; it is to be found in the old Spanish quarter around OLVERA STREET. The PLAZA DE ARMAS used to be the soldiers' parade ground, and there is also a church from this time. San Gabriel and Olvera Street, which once stood in a desolate wilderness, now find themselves amid a sea of houses in the third largest city in the USA.

The missions and the Presidios continued to be extended further north, with increased pressure from the mother country of Spain. The reason was that Russian fur traders from the region of Siberia were spreading across the Bering Straits to ALASKA. They had already established bases in the far north-west of the continent, on the Kodiak and ALEUTIAN ISLANDS, to start a lucrative trade with the Eskimos, Indians and Aleutians, a trade centred around the highly desirable and extremely expensive sea otter skins. The Spaniards assumed there was a danger of the Russians' advancing further southwards, if only on account of the milder climate; the fur traders needed agricultural land to provide for themselves, and in Alaska they could neither grow cereals nor keep cattle. There was yet another threat apart from the Russians, for in the summer of 1792 the energetic Scotsman Alexander Mackenzie succeeded in crossing the continent from east to west and reaching the Pacific coast near Bellacola, in what is now Canada. It was naturally to be feared that the British would penetrate into Spanish California. The Spaniards felt that they had to forestall this peril by establishing further settlements within the next few years; SAN JOSE in 1796, SAN MIGUEL and SAN JUAN in 1797, and then three more, the final one being SAN SOLANO, in 1822.

It was the end of a chain ingeniously planned to ensure that each mission lay a day's journey from the next, the distance between them therefore varying according to the terrain. The missions not directly situated on the coast had a cart track leading to the next safe anchorage, although it could often take up to six months before a ship would appear. Anyone placing an order or dispatching a letter to Spain found his patience sorely tried, for a reply – assuming one ever came – could take two years or more. Nevertheless, in many cases the long wait paid off, and has proved of benefit to at least some of the families' descendants ever since.

It must be explained that the reigning Spanish monarch was entitled to award gifts of land even in distant California, either as a recognition of loyal service or because the applicant swore future allegiance to the throne. No-one felt obliged to survey the land; it was sufficient to describe a range of mountains or the course of a river to define the borders and to make sure that nobody else had staked a claim there before. The possible presence of natives was quite immaterial. The best way to ensure success was to apply to the King of Spain in person. And so vast estates came into being in that long-past Spanish era, many of them larger than the old dukedoms of Europe; the GOLDEN AGE OF THE DONS had begun.

Many of the landowners never even explored the borders of their territory. Thanks to the fine grazing lands, the flocks of cattle, sheep, horses and donkeys multiplied into the uncountable. The Indios too, protected and cared for by the missions, increased their numbers until the friars found it difficult to employ all of them, and eventually some missions were populated by thousands of baptised Indians. As a rule the native people were also happy to provide cheap labour for the Dons, although this was no simple case of exploitation. No-one starved; there were more than ample foodstuffs of all kinds and the very poorest families had more horses, donkeys and mules than they could ever need. Anyone who felt so inclined could raid the herds of the nearest Don and remove a few sheep or calves for the cooking pot while the landowners looked benignly on.

What was really missing was a number of facilities that the simplest peoples would find necessary these days. In the whole of California there were neither schools nor teachers, not one doctor, dentist or hospital. It was left to the missionaries to deal with the sick and dying as best they could. Books were rare; good clothes were precious. All the requirements of daily life had to be produced on the spot, by the settlers in their homes, the Dons not excepted. There was plenty of wine, for instance, but no mugs or glasses to drink from. They had to be imported from Mexico or even from Spain, while the missions' vineyards prospered increasingly from year to year. So on the one hand the Californians were living a life of affluence that almost amounted to luxury, and on the other there was a sad lack of many things that we would consider indispensable today.

There was no serious threat to these communities from the north in the nineteenth century. The fear of a Russian advance was allayed when DON ANTONIO ARGUELLO, the Spanish governor of San Francisco, negotiated a peaceful solution over the heads of his superiors in Madrid and Mexico, and allowed ALEXANDER BARANOV, the imperial Russian governor of Alaska, several thousand acres of agricultural land near BODEGA BAY to grow crops and keep cattle and poultry, thus providing for the fur traders in the wilds of Alaska. The subjects of the Czar were quite happy with this arrangement and contented themselves with erecting a stronghold named FORT ROSS, to be manned by a mere sixty soldiers from distant Siberia. Their numbers were swelled by one hundred and fifty native fishermen from the Aleutian Islands, with their unmatched ability to trap the valuable Pacific sea otters.

The British too presented no threat, either to the peaceful life of California's communities or to the beneficial work of the missions, for they demanded no more than a few of their own trading posts at the mouth of the Columbia River. The real danger to California, which eventually led to a complete transformation of the land, came from Mexico. One of the reasons for this was the weakness of Spain in the face of the continuing threat from Napoleon. The Spanish government was no longer capable of administrating its oversized empire. Many, or rather most, of the Spanish colonies demanded independence, and the Viceroyalty of Mexico too became the scene of a rebellion against a viceroy who could not even be sure of the loyalty of his own troops. No sooner had one rebellion been quashed than another broke out somewhere else. It took almost twenty years of civil war in Mexico before independence from Spain was finally achieved.

This turmoil scarcely affected either California or its inhabitants. Events there took quite a different turn, for the governors of Monterey, San Francisco and Sacramento simply pronounced themselves independent. There were still very few Spaniards, but to a great extent they governed themselves. For the time being the missions carried on with their work, and even managed to consolidate their position up as far as Solano.

For a long time California remained isolated from the outside world. In the meantime Mexico had become independent and actually found itself an emperor, AUGUSTIN DE ITURBIDE by name, in the years 1822 and 1823. The rulers of Mexico, however, had not forgotten California completely, and governors were delegated to enforce laws, according to which the missions were to be closed down and handed over to the local Indians. Obviously, even the first attempts at dissolution brought disastrous results, for without the friars, the teachers and the daily routine, the natives were unable to keep up the running of the missions. As long as it was at all possible, the Franciscans, a number of Dons and, surprisingly, some of the governors from Mexico, tried to preserve the missions and the old way of life. Nevertheless, sixteen of the twenty-one had already been wound up by 1834. Five years later, all the missions were silent; their work was at an end. Anything that could be of use was looted, and corrupt government representatives sent from Mexico seized the lands either for themselves or for their friends and relations. Churches were turned into store houses; the roof tiles that the Indians had fashioned were removed and used elsewhere. (Only a few years ago someone who was renovating an old granary near San Diego discovered amidst all the rubble a well-preserved chapel, complete with its original altar that had been imported from Spain.) The nomads and the baptised Indians alike fell prey to diseases which outsiders had brought in and for which there was no cure; no-one bothered to provide for them any more and they sank into oblivion; few remain to this day.

As the missions closed down, so began a stream of illegal immigrants from America. Although both Spanish and Mexican law forbade all such settlers, the sections of the border that meandered along mountain ranges were virtually un-patrolled and immigrants could easily trickle in unnoticed by the authorities. By now, American trappers and dealers had reached the Wild West and in their wake came rogues, gangsters and outlaws. They had crossed the seas of prairie grass and, when they reached the stony foothills of the Rockies, knew very well that beyond lay the fertile valleys, pastures and forests of California, a beautiful and, it was rumoured, wealthy land that belonged to Mexico but was in a state of permanent civil war, with no proper government but only a few local administrators. With this in mind the first "mountainmen" crossed the Rockies in 1826, set up their traps and started trading with the Indians. On occasions they took advantage of the Dons' inability to defend themselves adequately. There were raids and lootings, the Ranchos were plundered and only too often the owner murdered. If the guilty were brought to justice, perhaps landing in a Mexican jail, the American government only had to protest and the culprits were set free, a fact that became common knowledge both among the American adventurers and the European immigrants. In long trails of covered wagons more and more land-hungry families broke through hostile Indian country and, often with terrible loss of life, conquered the heights and depths of the Rocky Mountain range. There was enough room for everyone over there, on the sunny side, and at first the settlers simply seized any land that they fancied; even if it was already someone else's property, there was no court to handle such disputes.

A comparison of school history books in the USA and in Mexico will soon reveal two completely different points of view about what was now to happen. California had so much to offer but was only sparsely populated by whites; it was self-evident to the Americans that they should consider it their "manifest destiny" that California by rights belonged to them and that they alone were capable of developing its enormous potential – which admittedly they did. With this aim, an indefinite number of agents, trouble-makers and rabble-rousers were sent into the country in an undercover operation designed to provoke all possible revolt and thus gain freedom from Mexican rule.

The example of Texas illustrates only too clearly what was destined to happen in California, for Texas, with its wide expanses of thinly populated land, had also once been a part of Mexico. Then so many American immigrants flooded in, illegally as everyone knew, that the few Mexicans and even fewer Spanish settlers soon found themselves in the minority. The resulting rebellion of the "Yanquis" led in no time to the proclamation of the Free Republic of Texas, which within a few years applied for admission to the USA. This request was, naturally enough, granted, but since the Mexican President was short-sighted enough to dispute the decision, full-scale war broke out with the USA in 1846. Pitched against the might of the United States, the Mexicans with their meagre resources were doomed to utter defeat, although they put up an astounding fight. In the ensuing Peace of HIDALGO GUADELUPE, Mexico was forced to cede about half its territory to the

USA; that included the present states of New Mexico, Arizona, Nevada, Utah, parts of Colorado and, as was to be expected, the whole of California. With the aid of the American occupation forces, a provisional government was soon set up in California, and this body requested, as planned, entry into the United States of America. Washington gracefully granted her permission.

The discovery of gold in Sacramento valley immediately after the American occupation provided the real explosive material that opened up the whole state to rapid development. It has been reckoned that no less than sixty thousand Americans greedy for gold found their way to California either over the prairies or via the dreaded sea route around Cape Horn. Although only a handful of the prospectors struck lucky, and usually lost their fortunes just as rapidly as they had found them, it was inevitable that the large number of immigrants streaming in would change California within a few years. The families of Spaniards and Mexicans found themselves pushed aside if they did not come to an agreement with the new authorities. The rare Indians who had survived disease, exploitation and expulsion disappeared from view. Most of the Dons, who had been the only landowners till now, were simply dispossessed of all they had, and a whole class that had enjoyed social and cultural prominence saw itself driven into isolation and deprived of power. In spite of, or perhaps just because of that, the few such families who have survived to this day lay great emphasis on keeping their little circle as exclusive as possible.

These days there are an increasing number of "Latinos" in California, as a result of legal, and more often illegal, immigration from Mexico. Occasionally one sees "Ami go home" scrawled on walls, but the Americans are here to stay, for they have made California what it is today.

It took a few decades of unrest before the state settled down to anything approaching a peaceful and orderly existence. Soon industry was flourishing, and to this there is still no end in sight. The former estates of the Franciscan missions burgeoned into a turmoil of cities. SAN FRANCISCO was the first of any importance, then MONTEREY, which became the capital. In 1854, however, SACRAMENTO was made capital of California and has remained so ever since. In the second half of the last century there were once again stirrings from the Franciscan order, who had already had some of their missions returned to them by President Lincoln. Ruins underwent painstaking restoration, although only one, San Luis Rey, has been able to resume its original task of welfare work among the Indians, and this not in the old mission buildings but in the nearby PALA RESERVATION. Other former missions have become schools or seminaries for priests, often with their own museum, and almost all the churches are once again used for religious purposes.

California was hardly touched by the Civil War of 1862 – 1866. It remains the most popular state for immigrants in the USA; the wagon train still rolls on. Any further obstacle to California's development was finally overcome when a railway was constructed from coast to coast and a direct train service started from New York to San Francisco in 1873. Raw materials were discovered in abundance, among them apparently inexhaustible supplies of oil. Newly-founded industries expanded into positions of increasing significance, and, when the local work force became unable to cope, as happened in the first instance with railroad construction, thousands of Chinese were imported to help out. Japanese, Philipinos and Indonesians followed. Their descendants have multiplied industriously and are surely a boon to this huge land. San Francisco has the largest of these bustling and extensive Chinatowns.

Canyons and Indians

The agreeable climate and above all the long hours of sunshine attracted the filmmakers soon after the invention of cinematography. Today HOLLYWOOD is a well-established tradition and its studios extend over many miles. A visit can always be arranged and is well worth it. DISNEYLAND near Los Angeles really needs more than a day's visit. Then there is the QUEEN MARY, once the biggest and most luxurious ocean liner of the seven seas, which now lies off Los Angeles and has been turned into a floating museum, restaurant and hotel. Not only tourists but even Californians themselves are speechless with amazement when they visit the so-called MARINELANDS that are to be found along the coast from San Diego to San Francisco and beyond. Blonde girls ride upon the backs of killer whales and the whales themselves delight the public with their tricks. The only live koala bears outside Australia are to be found in San Diego Zoological Gardens, and just as remarkable are the hundred or so species of penguin who have been provided with a complete Antarctic biotope behind massive glass walls. Even the light conditions resemble those of the South Polar seas, and happily this has encouraged the penguins to mate and produce young. One of the newest and most valuable museum collections in the world is to be found in the unique MALIBU MUSEUM near Los Angeles. The famed Paul Getty, having made his billions in oil, presented the building and its priceless contents to the public; admission is free, but you are advised to book in advance.

California, the state overflowing with riches and fortune, is of course blessed with a plentiful supply of museums, art collections and foundations. One of these is SAN SIMEON, erected by the American press lord and magnate of the film industry, William Randolph Hearst. His fantastic creation lies above the Big Sur near the Camino Real and comprises a whole collection of castles filled with art treasures from all over the world. Many sections of the buildings have been brought by sea from antique lands and eastern countries and then transported overland to San Simeon to be fitted into new facades. They stand in broad acres of well-kept parkland and the effect is not always in the best of taste, but San Simeon is indisputably a valuable collection and well worth seeing: what Hearst's overflowing inventiveness and immeasurable fortune achieved here is almost beyond belief. The HUNTINGDON MUSEUM in Los Angeles is rather more tastefully furnished than San Simeon and has a collection that is possibly of even better quality and of more value. It is set in a few square miles of botanical gardens that contain the most varied collection of cacti in the world – or so they say.

Anyone who is so enthusiastic about California as to want to visit all the museums worth seeing would have to begin in the New Year to be home by Christmas. Part of the reason is that a lot of the museums are in remote areas, especially those with private collections. I had great difficulty, for example, in finding the SOUTHWEST MUSEUM, whose name reveals nothing of the fact that it houses a collection illustrating aspects of Indian culture.

An experience not to be missed is that of crossing the bridge spanning an artificial arm of the Colorado River close to LAKE HAVASU CITY. This construction of solid granite is over one hundred and fifty years old and was officially opened by King William IV of Great Britain on May 1st 1835 – only at that time it happened to span the Thames. A century passed and the bridge was found inadequate to deal with the traffic, so it was demolished and the material, all one hundred and fifty thousand tons of it, sold to an enterprising businessman who was in the process of converting a stretch of semi-desert on the sun-baked borders of California, containing only scrub and prickly pears, into a town for senior citizens. At least the land was going for a song. The sensational transfer of the old London Bridge was to provide a status symbol and publicity for the project. Since there was unfortunately no water for the bridge to cross, some had to be provided, and the nearby Colorado was brought to the rescue. The publicity stunt of erecting the old London Bridge over Havasu Creek cost five million dollars.

Up and down the coast, wherever bays and breakwaters are to be found, innumerable yachts and cruisers lie at anchor, of every shape and size, from the severely functional to the extravagantly luxurious. Fine holiday weather will find the blue-green water a mass of boats, too many boats, spreading far out to sea. There are islands and groups of islands, the CATALINAS for example, where rare animals, above all birds, enjoy such a degree of protection that they allow people to approach them within a few yards. There is no lack of bathing beaches, dance halls or casinos either, nor of the usual flocks of tall slim girls wearing little or next to nothing to cover their immaculate suntan. In certain streets, normally in the suburbs of the big cities – the incredibly long winding SUNSET BOULEVARD in Los Angeles, for example – there is a teeming mass of hippies, punks, homos, hermanas and people with whatever other names these "freaks" like to call themselves. Not a few are decked out from head to foot in glittering chains and other baubles and have draped over their shoulders live squirrels or droll little rats with large yellow incisors. Actually they are harmless, both people and animals, and extraordinarily friendly in the bargain.

As a complete contrast we can turn to the world-famous holiday resorts of the upper ten thousand. PALM SPRINGS is supposedly one of these superior areas; here the richest and most successful Americans spend their time in spring, autumn and often in winter too. They are, however, rarely to be seen. Their seldom luxurious and mostly one-storey houses are hidden in large overgrown gardens and they practise their own form of apartheid in that they only mix with each other and even play golf in their own golf clubs.

There were very few settlements or effective missions in NEW MEXICO, ARIZONA, NEVADA, COLORADO or UTAH at that time, but despite this there was a considerable, if indirect, influence from Spain, traces of which have survived into our own time. The domestic animals which brought such changes to the lives of the natives all came from the Spanish and Mexicans. The silverwork and the blanket weaving that were developed into a real art by the Navajo and the Hopi are also legacies of the Spanish age.

Approximately a tenth of Arizona still belongs to, or rather has been restored to, the Indians. Some time ago the American government granted the NAVAJO and the HOPI almost complete jurisdiction over their reservations. These two tribes have always been far more civilised than the indigenous tribes of California, who lived in the most primitive conditions. As a result of the bloody Indian wars and the subsequent expulsion of the tribes from their traditional territory, the Navajos were reduced to under seven thousand half-starved survivors; within one hundred years their numbers have increased to nearly 200,000 and they are once more in possession of their old tribal lands. Their numbers are still steadily growing, although the Hopi have scarcely doubled their population within the same time. There are about 3,000 Hopi living in a relatively small reservation which is completely surrounded by the vast Navajo territory. Navajo and Hopi are nevertheless two unrelated peoples with different languages and with quite different customs.

A great number of the natural wonders of the American Southwest are to be found in Monument Valley, as a study of the photographs in our book will reveal. Originally there was a plateau here, 5,000 feet high; in the course of millions of years, water, ice and melting snow have washed away most of the softer rock, while leaving the harder layers far less eroded. These remain in bizarre shapes, towering pillars and gigantic cave mouths; it is like being in a dream world, where wonder after wonder assails one's vision, and at the end of it all one has still seen only a small part of this miraculous landscape.

The Canyon de Chelly, also within the Navajo reservation, is inhabited by a few hundred families during the summer. Many of them live in the very same sort of hogans that were once the homes of their forefathers hundreds or even thousands of years ago. Hogans are hexagonal, sometimes octagonal, huts made of solid tree trunks and roofed with mud or turf. Chelly Canyon snakes for miles through steep cliff walls. Another of its sights are the caves with their cliff dwellings; when they were inhabited is uncertain but they contain a number of well-preserved wall paintings with indecipherable symbols.

Some of these cliff castles are hundreds of yards wide. They were built deep into caves in vertical cliff faces and are to be found in the ravines of the Mesa plateau. The Mesa reaches heights of over 8,000 feet and its name derives from a Spanish word meaning "table", used here to describe a plateau or tableland that is slashed by steep-sided valleys. The cave dwellers of old lived on food from their fields and on wild plants from the ravines; in times of danger they needed only to scurry up the narrow ladders into their caves, where defence was not difficult. Here they had a stock of provisions, with cool springs to provide water. Some cliff dwellings contain about two hundred and fifty walled rooms. Carbon dating has shown that the Mesa culture blossomed from the beginning of the eleventh century till the middle of the fourteenth; the cliff dwellers belonged to the ancient tribe of the Anasazi. It is not known for certain why they abandoned the Mesa.

Utah can also boast a large number of natural wonders, and luckily the authorities have been far-sighted enough to enclose them in protected areas before it is too late. The extraordinary number of natural bridge formations fall into this category. In ARCHES NATIONAL PARK there are no fewer than 89 of them; their shapes have been scoured out over millions of years by water erosion and they span valleys that can be anything up to one hundred and fifty feet wide and just as deep. Some bridges are so thin and narrow at the top of the arch that it takes courage to walk across; the really daring can try it on horseback.

Such structures as these have been formed over millions of years, and of course the process never stops. BRYCE CANYON, in the south-west of Utah, is yet another of nature's miracles that has absolutely no equal, a deserted wilderness from which rise jagged towers of stone that glow red at dawn and dusk. Although it seems so inaccessible, Bryce Canyon was actually discovered by Spanish friars, who cautioned others to avoid this savage landscape. In 1821, American fur dealers arrived here and half a century later some settlements were founded by MORMONS in 1864.

Everyone knows the greatest tourist attraction of the Southwest to be the GRAND CANYON, where the Colorado flows through an enormous ravine up to a mile deep in places. One of the wonders of the world, it was discovered as early as 1542 by LOPE DE CARDENAS, a member of Francisco Coronado's expedition. Even the most professional photographs of the Grand Canyon cannot attempt to capture the ever-changing effects of the light at sunrise and sunset.

Something that for me surpasses the Grand Canyon itself is HAVASU VALLEY, the comparatively little-known home of the HAVASUPAI INDIANS. Their name means approximately "green water people" and they live in a narrow valley of no great length, which is filled with luxuriant vegetation. This is their reservation and a restricted number of visitors are allowed in at the Indians' discretion. If you are lucky enough to be granted permission to descend, the best form of transport is undoubtedly a mule; one of the conditions of entry is that absolutely no litter at all may be left in the valley.

Since California and its neighbouring states encompass such a wide variety of landscapes, from dusty deserts to snow-covered mountain ranges, not forgetting eight hundred miles of Pacific coastline, weather forecasting is a somewhat haphazard and unreliable procedure; the sun can be baking hot in Death Valley while at the same time snow is blocking the entrance to Sequoia Park.

On the last day of my journey, you must imagine me waiting for a flight from BORREGO SPRINGS to Los Angeles, from where I shall be able to board a plane that will take me to the terminal at Frankfurt and then on home to dear old Munich. The plane, an eight-seater Cessna – after all, it's only a short run to LA – fails to appear, although its imminent arrival is announced every few minutes. The pocket-sized airfield at Borrego has only one man in charge, and he eventually announces that thick fog is holding up the machine, as usual, and that there will have to be a diversion. Another passenger is waiting, just as impatient as I am, a tall, rather elderly man with a face that radiates vitality. At the moment he looks pretty disgruntled but still his eyes reveal that inner energy.

"It's always the same in this country, "he grumbles. "Try and get from here to LA – it's easier to fly to the moon. Now there's a punctual take-off for you, and, brother, you land right on time."

I was just about to start laughing at this ludicrous remark when the man behind the counter looked over warningly at me.

"The gentleman's not joking", he confided to me. "He should know what he's talking about. That's Neil Armstrong, the first man on the moon . . . remember July 21st, 1969 ?"

Wunderbares Kalifornien

Wer drüben Kalifornien sagt, meint sehr viel mehr als nur den Bundesstaat dieses Namens. Der Begriff Kalifornien ist grenzüberschreitend und schließt so ungefähr alles ein, was seinerzeit die Spanier entdeckt, erforscht oder auch nur berührt haben. Es hat ja all das noch, wenigstens auf dem Papier, bis 1848 zu Mexiko gehört.

Die ans eigentliche Kalifornien grenzenden Gebiete sind klimatisch, geologisch und auch landschaftlich dem heutigen US-Staat Kalifornien eng verwandt. Weshalb es mir durchaus vertretbar erscheint, daß wir sie in diesen Bildband einbeziehen. Wohl jedem Besucher wird es gleichfalls so ergehen. Man darf es nicht so eng sehen wie auf Landkarten.

Alles hat Kalifornien zu bieten, was sich der Mensch nur wünschen kann auf dieser Erde. Mildes Klima, guten Boden und zweihundertfünfzig Sonnentage im Jahresdurchschnitt. Sandige Badestrände und wildromantische Küsten wechseln ab. Schneebedeckte Berge, tiefgrüne Wälder und sagenhaft schöne Täler, alles ist da. Auch weite und windige Hochflächen, die sich zur rechten Zeit in Blütenmeere verwandeln. Dornbuschsteppen breiten sich aus, Kakteenwälder und Palmenoasen mit frischen Quellen. Bezaubernde Seen jeder Form und Farbe, viele davon eingebettet in Gebirge, die hinaufreichen bis zum ewigen Eis. Alles ist vorhanden im wunderbaren Kalifornien.

Weil die Landschaft von Kalifornien und der angrenzenden Regionen so verschieden ist, weil staubige Wüsten ebenso dazugehören wie eisgekrönte Gebirge, dazu zweitausend Kilometer pazifische Küste, kann sich niemand aufs Wetter verlassen. Auch nicht aufs amtlich angesagte Wetter. Während im Todestal glühend heiß die Sonne brennt, kann brausender Schneesturm die Zufahrt in den Sequoia-Park blockieren.

Dieser drittgrößte Staat der USA dehnt sich am Pazifischen Ozean über 1250 Kilometer aus und über zehn Längengrade, während vom Meer bis zur Grenze die Breite 230 bis nahe 1000 Kilometer beträgt. Somit umfaßt das Riesengebiet 411 000 Quadratkilometer, im Vergleich die Bundesrepublik nur 249 000 Quadratkilometer. Während aber unsere Bevölkerung fast sechzig Millionen erreicht, sind es im viel größeren Kalifornien erst 22 Millionen. Aber sie nehmen zu von Jahr zu Jahr, dank der lebhaften Einwanderung aus den übrigen Staaten der USA und (meist illegal) aus Mexiko.

In Kalifornien, dem Land der Superlative, erhebt sich der höchste Berg der Vereinigten Staaten (ausgenommen Alaska), der Mount Whitney, mit 4418 Metern. Auch die tiefste Stelle von ganz Amerika, knapp 90 Meter unter dem Meeresspiegel, befindet sich in Kalifornien, nahe Badswater im Todes-Tal. Mit 7700 Quadratkilo-metern ist auch das heiße, staubtrockene Deathvalley eines der Naturschutzgebiete. „Parks" und „Nationalparks" werden sie genannt, sind aber das Gegenteil von gepflegten Gartenlandschaften. Man will sie stattdessen so weit wie irgend möglich im Naturzustand belassen.

Viel hat einer zu tun, der alle Superlative des Landes sehen möchte, und weit klaffen die Gegensätze auseinander. Die stärksten, die höchsten und die ältesten Bäume der Welt sind in Kalifornien zu sehen. Im Methusala-Park an der Grenze zu Nevada stehen viele Dutzend von zerzausten Borstenzapfenkiefern, die schon gelebt haben, als der Pharao Cheops mit dem Bau seiner Pyramide begann.

Aktive Vulkane gibt es in Kalifornien, die gelegentlich in die Luft fliegen und weite Gebiete verwüsten, wie unlängst der Mount Helen im Staat Washington. Auch Erdbeben sind nicht selten, eines mit nachfolgender Feuersbrunst hat vor rund achtzig Jahren San Francisco zerstört.

So gut wie alles gedeiht in Kalifornien. Auch jede Art von Südfrüchten, im achtzehnten Jahrhundert von spanischen Missionaren eingeführt, hat sich prächtig entwickelt. Den rechten Boden für fast jede Sorte und das passende Klima gibt es nicht nur in einer Region des gesegneten Kalifornien, sondern in vielen. Was auch immer die Pioniere mitbrachten aus dem alten Europa und fernen Winkeln der Welt, hat sich aufs beste vermehrt. Dazu gehören auch die vorher in Amerika unbekannten Haustiere wie Schafe, Rinder, Ziegen, Pferde, Esel und so weiter. Nicht zu vergessen das Federvieh jeder nur denkbaren Art. Die Truthähne allerdings, die waren schon da, die sind umgekehrt von Mittelamerika zu uns gekommen.

Bis heute nicht erschöpft ist des Landes Reichtum an Gold, Silber, Kupfer, Öl und sonst noch vielbegehrten Rohstoffen. Ein relativ dichtes Netz guter Straßen durchzieht das sehenswerte Land. Vierspurig, auch fünfspurig sind die Autobahnen, aber nicht rascher als sechzig Meilen (sechsundneunzig Stundenkilometer) darf man fahren.

Die schönste Straße Kaliforniens, genannt „Traumstraße der Welt", ist die Bundesstraße Nr. 1, besser bekannt unter den Namen BIG SUR. Davon der beste, mit nichts anderem zu vergleichende Abschnitt verläuft nahe der Küste zwischen Monterey und der Morro-Bay. Hinauf und hinab, um Felsnasen herum führt der Weg. Allenthalben ist höchste Vorsicht geboten, aber gerade hier wird der Fahrer zum Luxus der Langsamkeit gezwungen. Nach jeder Wendung eine neue Sensation wilder Schönheit. Ein Kaleidoskop von Felsen und Farben, von hochschlagender Brandung, sanft auslaufenden Wellen und Seegrasfeldern, die im Wasser schweben. Inseln so hoch und steil wie Kirchtürme ragen aus dem Meer, tiefe Buchten erinnern an norwegische Fjorde. Die gesamte Region des BIG SUR ist menschenleer wie keine andere Region Kaliforniens.

Chapparal bedeckt nach wie vor die über der Big-Sur-Straße liegenden Berge, eine Dornbuschwildnis, die sich weder für Schafe noch Rinder eignet, erst recht nicht für Felder, Äcker und Gemüsebau. Deshalb sind lange Zeit keine Siedler gekommen. Dem ersten, der um das Jahr 1880 erschien, einem Deutschen namens Pfeifer, gelang es aber doch, sein Auskommen zu finden. Noch tüchtiger waren seine zahlreichen Nachbarn, denen die Erschließung der Gegend zu verdanken ist. Viele Ortschaften, Berge und Flüsse sind nach den Pfeifers genannt. Das meiste hat danach William Randolph Hearst nahe der Küste und weit droben in den Bergen geschaffen, nämlich eine fabelhafte Ansammlung von Schlössern, Museen und Parks, SAN SIMEON genannt. Über 1000 Millionen von den guten alten Dollars soll dafür der Pressezar und Beherrscher von Hollywood verbraucht haben.

Als Wohltat für Touristen erweisen sich die zahlreichen VISTAPOINTS mit ihren Parkplätzen. Man findet solche Rundblicke auf Landspitzen über dem Meer. Wer Geduld hat und ein gutes Glas vor Augen, sieht Seelöwen und Seehunde, entdeckt sogar See-Elefanten am Strand. Draußen erkennt man womöglich Pottwale, Grauwale und sogar den Blauwal, das größte Tier der Welt. Unvergeßlich der Anblick von Seeottern. Weil man die herrlich schönen, harmlosen Tiere der kostbaren Felle wegen lange Zeit gnadenlos verfolgt hat, galten sie gegen Ende des vorigen Jahrhunderts als restlos ausgerottet. Aber wunderbarerweise sind im Jahre 1937 einige wieder aufgetaucht. Seitdem – streng geschützt und bewacht – haben sich die Seeotter bis heute auf weit über hunderttausend Tiere vermehrt.

Was die Menschen betrifft, vor allem die Einwanderer aus den USA und Europa, so war auch deren Fortschritt kaum zu bremsen. Die meisten Kalifornier, äußerlich betrachtet, befinden sich bei guter Gesundheit, sind hochgewachsen, frisch und leicht beweglich. Allerdings halten sie viel von sich selber und blicken frohgemut in die Zukunft. Kritik an ihrem Land und seinen Leuten vertragen sie nicht. Kalifornien, der einunddreißigste und der volkreichste Staat der USA geht ihnen über alles, über alles in der Welt!

Vier großartige, gut gepflegte Nationalparks bestehen allein in Kalifornien, weitere achtzehn Gebiete hat man durch Sondergesetze vor dem Verderben bewahrt. Unsereins, der aus dem übervölkerten, weitgehend zugebauten Europa kommt, kann nur staunen über soviel, was schon so lange die Kalifornier wirkungsvoll für ihre Umwelt getan haben.

Die Geschichte des Süd-Westens der USA

Angefangen hat alles mit den Spaniern, auch wenn es seinerzeit nur sehr wenige waren, die von Mexiko aus in den Nordwesten vorgedrungen sind. Aber ihr Baustil, ihre Gartenkunst, die von ihnen eingeführten Kulturpflanzen und Haustiere sind heute noch dominierend im ganzen Land. Den Maultierpfaden der Missionare folgen manche der Autobahnen unserer Tage. Aus den damals angelegten Missionen sind die heute von Millionen Menschen bevölkerten Städte hervorgegangen. Deswegen haben sie ohne Ausnahme spanische Namen, und zwar nach Heiligen der Katholischen Kirche.

Entdeckt, sogar am südlichsten Rand erforscht, wurde Kalifornien schon um das Jahr 1535 von HERNANDO CORTEZ selber, dem Eroberer und Vizekönig von Mexiko. Aber es geschah nicht im heute amerikanischen Kalifornien, sondern in Niederkalifornien, an der noch heute zu Mexiko gehörenden, etwa tausend Kilometer langen, relativ schmalen Halbinsel Baja California. Aber der Versuch, so früh schon jene ferne Gegend zu besiedeln, mußte scheitern. Stattdessen haben kühne Seefahrer den Verlauf der Küste erforscht und sind am Ende weit hinauf bis nach Kanada gekommen, ja vielleicht bis Alaska. Vermutlich war es HERNANDO DE ALARCON, der als erster Europäer um 1540 den heutigen US-Staat Kalifornien betreten hat. Aber nirgendwo sind zu jener Zeit die Spanier ins Land vorgestoßen. Viel zu groß war damals schon das spanische Weltreich. Die Kräfte des Mutterlandes genügten nicht, um zugleich noch Kalifornien zu besetzen. Allein die sturmgeschützte Bucht von MONTEREY war wichtig für die Spanier als Zwischenstation für ihre Handelsflotte, die zweimal im Jahr zwischen dem Hafen ACAPULCO an der mexikanischen Westküste und MANILA, Hauptstadt der spanischen Phillipinen verkehrte.

Im übrigen sagte man seinerzeit LAS CALIFORNIAS, sprach also in der Mehrzahl vom Land Kalifornien. Ein riesengroßes Gebiet war damit gemeint, die gesamte Küste wie das noch unbekannte Hinterland, von Baja California im Süden bis hinauf nach Norden, soweit jemals ein spanisches Schiff gesegelt war. Fest glaubten die Spanier, daß alle diese Territorien der Krone von Spanien gehörten.

Erst um das Jahr 1700 begann zielbewußt die Erforschung, zur selben Zeit auch die Erschließung von Kalifornien. Mit LA PAZ an der Südspitze von Niederkalifornien wurde um das Jahr 1691 die erste Mission und 1822 nördlich der San-Francisco-Bucht mit SAN SOLANO die letzte Mission eingerichtet. Als 1770 der Franziskanerpater Junipero Serra die an der St.-Lucia-Bay gelegene Mission Carmel gegründet hat, lebten dort nur wenige hundert Nomaden, und sie standen noch auf der tiefsten Stufe menschlicher Entwicklung. Alles in allem bildeten die Missionen eine Kette von fast zweitausend Kilometern (in der Luftlinie), bestehend aus einunddreißig Missionen, jene von Baja California mitgerechnet. Ein bewundernswertes, für damalige Zeit gewaltiges Werk. Insgesamt einundzwanzig Missionen wurden im heutigen US-Staat Kalifornien angelegt, alle auf dem Landweg miteinander verbunden. Aber wie begreiflich ist, konnte man sich auf dem „Camino Real" (dem Königsweg) nur mit rumpelnden Ochsenkarren, Pferden und Maultieren bewegen. In der Mehrzahl aber waren es Fußgänger, meist mit schweren Lasten bepackt. In Niederkalifornien, in Baja California, sind während der letzten Jahrzehnte die meisten Stationen verfallen, nur stellenweise ist vom Camino Real noch etwas zu sehen. Vergebens habe ich versucht, ein paar Kilometer weit darüberzuwandern. Im US-Staat Kalifornien dagegen sind alle Missionen noch oder wieder vorhanden. Nicht im alten, im absolut echten Zustand, aber so gut restauriert, daß sie spürbar die damalige Stimmung ausstrahlen. Vieles von der Einrichtung blieb erhalten und kann betrachtet werden. So auch jene Gasträume, die für Offiziere und Regierungsbeamte reserviert waren. Es gibt Kirchen und Kapellen mit Altären, wo noch Pater Junipero Serra, Begründer der ersten Missionen, gepredigt hat. Deutlich können Besucher an der Anlage erkennen, wie es damals zuging und welche Aufgabe die einzelne Mission zu erfüllen hatte. Nicht nur ging es darum, die Seelen heidnischer Indianer durch christliche Taufe vor der Verdammnis zu retten, man wollte sie instand setzen, sich aus eigener Kraft zu erhalten, sich sozial zu verbessern und weiterzuentwickeln. Selber waren die Ureinwohner Kaliforniens kaum imstande, ihren Hunger zu stillen und sich feindlicher Menschen wie Tiere zu erwehren. Also kein Vergleich mit den Mayas und Azteken in Mexiko, auch nicht mit den Pueblo-Indianern und Mesabewohnern.

Sechs, sieben oder acht Völkerschaften sind seinerzeit durchs Land gezogen, jeweils mit verschiedenen Sprachen und Brauchtum. Aus hinterlassenen Berichten der Missionare geht hervor, daß sie sehr ängstlich, scheu und dann fügsam waren. Freiwillig kamen sie zu den Patres und Fratres, weil sie in den Missionen vor ihren Feinden geschützt waren, ein Dach über dem Kopf hatten und ausreichend ernährt wurden. Bei den ihnen übertragenen Arbeiten, beim Erlernen neuer Fähigkeiten zeigten sich große Unterschiede der Intelligenz wie auch des guten Willens. Manche brachten es zu Hufschmieden, zu Töpfern und Webern, sogar zur Kunst des Lesens, Schreibens und Rechnens. Andere konnten zeitlebens nur für einfachste Handarbeit gebraucht werden. Doch gab es auch Stämme und Stammesgruppen, die allen Versuchen der Bekehrung widerstanden. Es kam vor, daß sie die Missionen überfielen und die wehrlosen Franziskaner erschlugen. Deshalb war eigentlich vorgesehen, daß zu jeder Station ein PRESIDIO gehörte, eine aus zehn bis zwölf spanischen Soldaten bestehende und von einem Offizier geführte Schutzmacht. Aber es gab oft Schwierigkeiten zwischen den Mönchen und dem Militär. Die rauhen, meist jungen Soldaten stellten den Mädchen nach, betranken sich an dem für

die Messe angebauten Wein und gaben auch sonst den indianischen Taufkindern ein schlechtes Beispiel. Weshalb die frommen Franziskaner darauf drangen, daß die „Presidios", ebenso die Wohnplätze der Siedler, einige Meilen von der Mission und ihren Schäflein entfernt lagen. Aber wenn sodann ein Überfall der wilden Indios auf die Mission erfolgte, kamen die Soldaten zu spät.
Aber schließlich und endlich gelang es dem Franziskanerorden, aus Naturmenschen gute Mitarbeiter zu machen. Manche der getauften Indianer entwickelten echt künstlerische Fähigkeiten. In vielen der Missionen bewundern wir heute noch indianische Malereien und Schnitzereien, die deutlich eigenen Stil beweisen. Alle Stationen erhielten sich selbst. Sämtliche Notwendigkeiten, die man brauchte, wurden in oder bei der Mission hergestellt. Mit der Zeit konnte man bestimmte Produkte wie Seifen und gegerbtes Leder, auch Wachskerzen und Knochenpulver nach Mexiko, ja sogar ins spanische Mutterland exportieren. Wer sich in einer der wiederhergestellten Stationen umsieht, wird erstaunt, sogar verblüfft sein über die Vielzahl der Werkstätten und Menge der landwirtschaftlichen Geräte, die erkennen lassen, wie sich alles sinngemäß ineinander gefügt hat.
Aber so ganz haben die geistlichen Erzieher der Moral ihrer Schäflein nicht getraut. Bei Dunkelwerden hat man alle jungen Mädchen und auch verheiratete Frauen, deren Männer abwesend waren, hinter verschlossenen Türen gehalten!

SAN DIEGO, hart an der Grenze zu Mexiko, war im Sommer 1769 die erste Mission des Franziskanerordens im heutigen Bundesstaat Kalifornien. Von Mexiko her über Land kam der Hauptmann Gaspar de Portola. Er wurde begleitet, wohl besser gesagt geführt, von dem unermüdlichen Pater Junipero Serra. Er war es gewesen, der auf unvorstellbar langen, schwierigen Wanderungen durch völlig unbekanntes Land erst einmal die möglichen Wege erforscht hatte. Zweihundertzwanzig Siedler spanischer Abstammung, die Kinder eingeschlossen, folgten den Missionaren und Soldaten auf dem Fuße. Alle möglichen Haustiere, auch das notwendige Saatgut und die wichtigsten Werkzeuge führten sie mit. Weil mit dem Verlust vieler, ja sogar mit dem Verschwinden aller Beteiligten zu rechnen war, kamen andere Gruppen von Siedlern, Soldaten und Missionaren auf drei Schiffen über See. Während auf dem Landweg ein Drittel aller Menschen zugrunde gingen, erreichten von den drei Seeschiffen zwei die Bucht von San Diego. Unterwegs waren aber mehr als die Hälfte der Mannschaften wie auch der Mitreisenden an Hunger, Durst und Krankheit gestorben.
Kaum war auf einfachste Weise die Mission San Diego etabliert, ging es weiter hinauf und hinein ins Unbekannte. Auf mühsamen Märschen über Stock und Stein, über Dorngestrüpp und Gebirgspässe schleppten sich Siedler und Soldaten nach

Norden, als Pfadfinder voran der Pater Junipero Serra. Hinter ihm polterten und quietschten die Ochsenkarren. Etwa zur selben Zeit versuchten zwei schwerfällige Seeschiffe das gleiche, vorher vereinbarte Ziel zu erreichen. Immer wurde das Vordringen von schweren Verlusten begleitet. Aber man war das gewohnt, und ein paar Dutzend kamen immer durch. So entstanden die Missionen und Stationen von CARLOS BORROMEO DE CARMELO und SAN ANTONIO DE PADUA sowie LUIS OBISPO, SAN JUAN CAPSTRANO, SANTA CLARA, SANTA BARBARA und viele andere. Dann im September 1771 SAN GABRIEL ARCANGEL. Um heute diese Mission zu finden, braucht man einen sehr genauen Stadtplan von Los Angeles. Denn verborgen mitten im Häusergewirr der Siebenmillionen-Stadt liegt die alte, gut wiederhergestellte Mission der Franziskaner. Den Kolonisten, den Siedlern mit ihren Familien und Tieren gaben der Capitano und Pater Serra einen mehrere Meilen von San Gabriel entfernten Platz zum Verbleiben. Das sündige Leben des Presidio sollte eben nicht das Bekehrungswerk der Franziskaner stören. Auch diese Keimzelle der heute bis hundert Kilometer breiten Stadt blieb erhalten. Es sind die altspanischen Winkel um die OLVERA STREET und die PLAZA DE ARMAS dem einstigen Exerzierplatz der Soldaten. Eine Kirche aus der Zeit gehört dazu. Damals in menschenleerer Einsamkeit gelegen, befinden sich nun San Gabriel und die Olvera-Straße inmitten des Häusermeeres der drittgrößten Stadt in den USA.

Die Ausdehnung der Missionen und Presidios in nördlicher Richtung hört nicht auf. Sie wurde von der Regierung des spanischen Mutterlandes dringender gewünscht als bisher. Da waren nämlich aus dem sibirischen Raum russische Pelzhändler über die Bering-See nach ALASKA gekommen. Sie hatten im Nordwesten von Amerika, auf der Kodiak-Insel und den ALEUTEN-INSELN Stützpunkte angelegt, um mit den Indianern, den Eskimos und Aleuten gewinnbringenden Handel zu treiben. Es ging dabei vor allem um die hochbegehrten, hochbezahlten Felle des Seeotters. Es bestand die Gefahr, daß die Russen weiter nach Süden vorstießen, schon des milden Klimas wegen. Sie konnten in Alaska weder Getreide anbauen noch Vieh halten. Also brauchten sie landwirtschaftlich nutzbaren Boden für ihre Versorgung. Es gab noch eine zweite Gefahr. Da war es im Sommer 1792 dem energischen Schotten Alexander Mackenzie gelungen, von Osten her die ganze Breite des Kontinents zu durchqueren. Im heutigen Kanada, nahe der Ortschaft Bellacola, hatte Mackenzie den Pazifischen Ozean erreicht. Also war zu befürchten, daß sich von dorther die Briten bis nach Spanisch Kalifornien ausbreiten würden. Beiden Gefahren wollten und mußten die Spanier zuvorkommen, weshalb binnen weniger Jahre weitere Missionen entstanden: SAN JOSÉ im Jahr 1796, SAN MIGUEL und SAN JUAN 1797, zwei andere in den folgenden Jahren und als letzte vonallen, am Ende der Kette, SAN FRANCISCO DE SOLANO im Jahr 1822.

Wohl der beste Gedanke war, daß schließlich jede Mission von der nächsten eine Tagesreise entfernt lag. Das richtete sich nicht nach dem Längenmaß, sondern nach der dafür erforderlichen Zeit. Befanden sich die Missionen nicht direkt am Meer, führte ein Karrenweg bis zum nächsten sicheren Ankerplatz. Aber es konnten Monate, oft auch ein halbes Jahr vergehen, bis wieder ein Schiff erschien. Wer im damaligen Kalifornien dies oder jenes in Spanien bestellte oder einen Brief dorthin sandte, mußte viel Geduld haben. Bis die Antwort, bis die Bestellung eintraf (wenn sie eintraf), vergingen zwei Jahre und vielleicht noch mehr.

Es war nämlich so, daß der jeweils regierende König von Spanien für sich das Recht in Anspruch nahm, Grundbesitz auch im fernen Kalifornien zu verschenken. Entweder als Belohnung für treue Dienste oder ganz einfach, weil der Antragsteller versprach, treue Dienste zu leisten. Es war nicht nötig, die Lage der Länderei zu vermessen, es genügte, einen Höhenzug oder den Verlauf eines Flusses zu beschreiben, um die gewünschten Grenzen anzudeuten. Hauptsache, kein anderer Bewerber erhob Anspruch auf die gleiche Gegend. Die vielleicht dort lebenden Eingeborenen spielten keine Rolle. Aber zu diesem Zweck mußte sich der Antragsteller, wollte er des Erfolges sicher sein, selber nach Spanien begeben und den gerade regierenden König selber sprechen. Auf diese Weise sind in den alten spanischen Zeiten riesig weite Latifundien entstanden, manche größer als Fürstentümer im alten Europa. Damit begann die GOLDENE ZEIT DER DONS.

Manche der Grundherren haben niemals die Grenzen ihres Besitzes umrundet. Ihre Herden aus Rindern, Schafen, Pferden und Eseln vermehrten sich dank der guten Weidegründe ins Unermeßliche. Auch die Zahl der Indios, von den Missionen beschützt und versorgt, nahmen zu, ohne daß die Patres genügend Platz und Arbeit für sie hatten. Tausende von getauften Indios bevölkerten so manche der Missionen. Auch für die Dons waren sie ebenso billige wie meist auch willige Hilfskräfte. Ausgebeutet wurden sie nicht. Niemand mußte hungern, denn Lebensmittel verschiedenster Art wurden im Überfluß gewonnen. Selbst die ärmsten Familien besaßen mehr Pferde, Esel und Maultiere, als sie brauchten. Wer wollte, konnte sich aus der Herde des nächsten Don ein paar Schafe oder Kälber holen zum Verbrauch in der eigenen Küche. Die Herdenbesitzer störte das nicht.

Was aber fehlte, waren all jene Dinge, die heute auch die einfachsten Menschen für lebenswichtig halten. Es gab in ganz Kalifornien keine Schule und keine Lehrer, keinen Arzt oder Zahnarzt, natürlich auch kein Hospital. Nur die Missionare kümmerten sich, so gut sie es konnten, um Kranke und Sterbende. Jedes Buch galt als Seltenheit, und gute Kleider waren sehr kostbar. Alles, was die Menschen, auch die Dons, fürs tägliche Leben brauchten, mußte im Haus, mußte von den Siedlern selbst hergestellt werden. Zwar fehlte es nicht an Wein, aber an Bechern und Gläsern, ihn zu trinken. Die mußte man aus Mexiko, sogar aus Spanien importieren, während der Wein bei allen Missionen gut und reichlich gedieh. So lebten einerseits die damaligen Kalifornier im Überfluß, sogar im Luxus. Andererseits litten sie bittere Not an vielen Dingen, die für unsere Begriffe ganz gewöhnlich sind.

Nicht aus dem Norden kamen zu Anfang des 19. Jahrhunderts die echten Gefahren. Es waren keineswegs die Russen aus Alaska, die man zu fürchten hatte. Mit denen konnte sich DON ANTONIO ARGUELLEO, der spanische Gouverneur von San Francisco, auf vollkommen friedliche Weise einigen. Ohne erst lange in Madrid oder nur in Mexiko nachzufragen, überließ er 1805 dem ALEXANDER BARANOW, dem Kaiserlich Russischen Gouverneur von Alaska, einige tausend Hektar guten Landes nahe der BODEGA-BUCHT. Dort konnten die Russen Landwirtschaft treiben, auch Vieh und Geflügel halten zur Versorgung der Pelzhändler droben im kargen Alaska. Mehr wollten die Untertanen des Zaren nicht. Sie begnügten sich mit der Anlage einer Festung, FORT ROSS genannt, und mit einer Besatzung von nur sechzig Soldaten aus dem fernen Sibirien. Dazu schickten sie noch hundertfünfzig Eingeborene aus den Aleuten an die kalifornische Küste, weil es niemand so gut wie die Fischer der Aleuten-Inseln verstanden, den wertvollen Seeotter zu fangen. Die Gefahr fürs friedliche Leben in Kalifornien, auch für das segensreiche Wirken der Missionen, kam auch nicht von den Briten. Die hatten sich mit einigen wenigen Handelsposten an der Mündung des COLUMBIA-RIVER begnügt. Die Gefahr und schließlich die Verwandlung von ganz Kalifornien kam vom Süden, sie kam aus Mexiko. Der Grund dafür war einerseits die Schwäche des zur gleichen Zeit von Napoleon bedrängten Mutterlandes Spanien. Die dortige Regierung war nicht mehr imstande, das viel zu große Kolonialreich weiter zu beherrschen. Manche, ja sogar die meisten der spanischen Kolonien wollten unabhängig sein. Also kam es auch im Vizekönigreich Mexiko zur Rebellion gegen den spanischen Vizekönig, der sich nicht mehr auf alle seine Truppen verlassen konnte. Kaum war ein Aufstand niedergeschlagen, brach irgendwo anders ein neuer aus. Fast zwanzig Jahre lang hat in Mexiko der Bürgerkrieg gedauert, bis endlich die Loslösung von Spanien erreicht war.

Von all dem wurde das Land Kalifornien, wurden auch die Kalifornier selber kaum berührt. Ganz im Gegenteil machten sich Gouverneure in Monterey, San Francisco und Sacramento selbständig. So gering die Zahl der Spanier noch immer war, sie regierten sich mehr oder weniger selber. So blieben vorerst die Missionen bei ihrer Aufgabe, haben sogar die Kette bis hinauf nach Solano ausgebaut.

Lange blieb Kalifornien isoliert von der Außenwelt. Dann jedoch erinnerten sich die Machthaber im selbständig gewordenen Mexiko, wo es von 1822 bis 1823 sogar einen Kaiser gab, AUGUSTIN DE ITURBIDE mit Namen, des kalifornischen Landes. Gouverneure kamen und brachten neue Gesetze mit. Danach sollten die Missionen aufgelöst und den dort lebenden Indianern übergeben werden. Wie sich denken läßt, hatte schon der Versuch, dies zu tun, verheerende Folgen. Ohne ihre Patres und Lehrmeister, ohne die gewohnte Ordnung konnten die Eingeborenen die bisherigen Betriebe nicht erhalten. Solange wie das noch irgendwie möglich war, versuchten die Franziskaner, teilweise auch einige Dons und sogar mexikanische Gouverneure, die Missionen wie überhaupt die alte Lebensform zu bewahren. Jedoch waren im Jahre 1834 schon sechzehn von den einundzwanzig Missionen liquidiert. Fünf Jahre später funktionierte keine mehr. Alles, was irgend jemand brauchen konnte, wurde verschleppt. Korrupte, aus Mexiko geschickte Regierungsvertreter übernahmen den Grundbesitz oder beschenkten ihre Freunde und Verwandten. Kirchen wurden in Lagerschuppen verwandelt, und man hat die von den Missionsindianern angefertigten Ziegel von den Dächern genommen und anderweitig verwendet. Erst vor wenigen Jahren, als man bei San Diego einen alten Getreideschuppen renovieren wollte, kam hinter Schutt und Abfall eine wohlerhaltene Kapelle zum Vorschein, komplett mit dem seinerzeit aus Spanien importierten Altar.

Durch eingeschleppte Krankheiten, gegen die es keine Mittel gab, und weil sich niemand mehr um ihre Versorgung kümmerte, starben und verdarben die getauften wie auch die noch in der Wildnis lebenden Indianer. Nur geringe Reste sind noch vorhanden.

Etwa zu gleicher Zeit begann die illegale Einwanderung von Amerikanern. An sich war allen Fremden nach spanischen wie auch nach mexikanischen Gesetzen das Betreten Kaliforniens verboten. Aber wo die Grenzen nur ungefähr über die Höhenlinie der Gebirge verliefen, wo es weit und breit keine Grenzkontrollen gab, konnte nach Kalifornien einsickern, wer immer wollte. Amerikanische Trapper und Pelzhändler hatten den Wilden Westen erreicht, mit ihnen und nach ihnen auch Gauner, Gangster und gesetzlose Banden. Sie hatten die Grasmeere der Prärien durchwandert und waren an den Rocky Mountains, am Fuß der Felsenberge eingetroffen. Dahinter, das wußten sie schon, lagen die fruchtbaren Täler, die Weidegründe und Wälder von Kalifornien. Ein schönes und, wie man sagte, sehr reiches Land, das zur Republik Mexiko gehörte. Aber dort herrschte permanenter Bürgerkrieg, in Kalifornien gab es keine richtige Regierung, nur ein paar örtliche Machthaber.

Also stiegen schon 1826 die ersten „Mountainmen" über die Rockys, stellten drüben ihre Fallen und handelten mit den Indios. Gelegentlich erschienen sie bei den

Dons, die kaum imstande waren sich zu wehren. Es kam zu Überfällen wie Plünderungen, Ranchos wurden ausgeraubt und nicht selten die Besitzer umgebracht. Wurden die Schuldigen gefaßt, vielleicht sogar in ein mexikanisches Gefängnis geworfen, protestierte die amerikanische Regierung, und schon waren die Räuber wieder frei. Das sprach sich herum bei amerikanischen Abenteurern, auch bei Einwanderern aus Europa. In langen Zügen von Planwagen durchzogen mehr und noch mehr landhungrige Familien die Sperrgürtel der Indianer und sodann überwanden sie unter oft schrecklichen Verlusten die Höhen und Tiefen der Rocky Mountains. Drüben, auf der anderen, der sonnigen Seite war Platz genug vorhanden. Während der ersten Zeit nahm sich jeder von den Zugereisten an Grund und Boden, was ihm gefiel. Auch wenn das schon jemandem gehörte, es gab kein Gericht, das etwas gegen die Landräuber unternehmen konnte.

Betrachtet man die Geschichte des Landes aus amerikanischer Sicht, wie in den Schulbüchern der USA, verlief sie wesentlich anders, als wenn sie von spanischen und mexikanischen Historikern beschrieben wird.
Weil Kalifornien so viel zu bieten hatte, aber nur sehr dünn von Weißen besiedelt war, hielten es die Amerikaner für ihre offenbare Vorbestimmung (manifest destiny), daß eigentlich Kalifornien ihnen gehörte. Nur sie waren imstande (und waren es wirklich), die großen Möglichkeiten voll zu entwickeln. Zu diesem Zweck wurde auf „verdeckte Weise" eine unbestimmte Zahl von Agenten, von Unruhestiftern und Wühlmäusen ins Land geschickt. Die sollten nach Möglichkeit Aufstände entfachen mit dem Ziel der Loslösung von Mexiko.

Was im schönen Kalifornien geschehen mußte, sah man bereits in Texas. Auch dieses weite, nur dünn besiedelte Land gehörte zur mexikanischen Republik. Aber so viele Amerikaner wanderten ein, illegal, wie jeder wußte, daß bald die Mexikaner, erst recht die Nachkommen spanischer Siedler, in der Minderheit waren. Ein Aufstand der „Yanquis" war die Folge, und schon wurde die „Freie Republik Texas" ausgerufen. Wenige Jahre später beantragte sie ihre Aufnahme in die „Vereinigten Staaten von Amerika", was auch geschah. Weil das aber der mexikanische Präsident nicht hinnehmen wollte, kam es im Jahre 1846 zum regelrechten Krieg mit den USA. Wie sich bei den Machtverhältnissen denken läßt, wurden trotz erstaunlich harten Widerstands die Mexikaner am Ende total besiegt. Im nachfolgenden Frieden von HIDALGO GUADELUPE mußte Mexiko etwa die Hälfte seines Staatsgebietes an die Vereinigten Staaten abtreten. Dazu gehörten die heutigen US-Staaten Neumexiko, Arizona, Nevada, Utah, Teile von Colorado und natürlich ganz Kalifornien. Mit Beihilfe der amerikanischen Besatzung entstand schon bald eine provisorische Regierung in Kalifornien. Diese bat, wie vorgesehen, um Aufnahme in die Vereinigten Staaten von Amerika, und großzügig hat Washington der Bitte entsprochen.

Die Entdeckung des Goldes im Sacramento-Tal, gleich nach der amerikanischen Okkupation, war sodann der eigentliche Zündstoff für die rasante Entwicklung des gesamten Landes. Man schätzt, daß über die Prärie und ebenso auf dem Seeweg um das gefürchtete Kap Horn nicht weniger als sechzigtausend goldhungrige Amerikaner nach Kalifornien kamen. Haben auch nur wenige der Goldgräber ihr Glück gemacht, um es in den meisten Fällen bald wieder zu verlieren, der Strom so vieler Einwanderer mußte binnen weniger Jahre ganz Kalifornien verändern. Die Spanier, Mexikaner und ihre Nachkommen sahen sich an die Wand gedrückt, sofern sie nicht mit den neuen Machthabern paktierten. Die geringen Reste der von Krankheit, Ausbeutung oder durch Vertreibung dezimierten Indianer sah man nicht mehr. Die meisten der Dons, die bisherigen Grundherren, wurden schlicht enteignet. Die bis dahin kulturell wie gesellschaftlich führende Schicht sah sich isoliert und entmachtet. Dennoch sind bis zum heutigen Tage noch einige von ihnen vorhanden, und durchaus betont achten sie auf die Exklusivität ihres kleinen Kreises.

Nachdem einige Jahrzehnte in Unruhe vergangen waren, herrschten wieder einigermaßen Recht und Ordnung im Land. Rasch blühte die Wirtschaft auf, und noch längst ist kein Ende des Fortschritts erkennbar. Aus den Missionen und Stationen der Franziskaner, aus den Presidios der Spanier und Mexikaner entwickelten sich turbulente Großstädte. SAN FRANCISCO war der erste Mittelpunkt, aber nicht die Hauptstadt. Auf MONTEREY folgte SACRAMENTO, und es ist bis heute die kalifornische Hauptstadt geblieben. In der zweiten Hälfte des vorigen Jahrhunderts rührte sich auch wieder der Franziskanerorden. Denn schon Präsident Abraham Lincoln hatte ihnen einige Missionen zurückgegeben. Aus den Ruinen ist vieles im alten Stil erstanden. Aber nur eines der Klöster, San Luis Rey, konnte wieder seine alte Aufgabe übernehmen, nämlich die Indianerfürsorge. Jedoch nicht mehr in der alten restaurierten Station, sondern in der nahegelegenen PALA-RESERVATION. Aus anderen der ehemaligen Missionen wurden Schulen und Priesterseminare, oft mit angeschlossenen Museen. Fast jede der früheren Kirchen dient wieder religiösen Zwecken.
Vom amerikanischen Bürgerkrieg 1862 bis 1866 wurde Kalifornien kaum berührt. Stattdessen war es und ist noch heute das meistbeliebte Einwanderungsland der USA. Als die erste Eisenbahn den gesamten Kontinent durchquerte, als schon 1873

Canyons und Indianer

direkte Züge von New York bis San Francisco rollten, gab es für die Entwicklung Kaliforniens kein Halten mehr. Rohstoffe in Hülle und Fülle wurden entdeckt, darunter Erdöl in unerschöpflicher Menge. Industrien entstanden, dehnten sich aus und gewannen immer größere Bedeutung. Weil einheimische Arbeitskräfte nicht genügten, zunächst beim Bahnbau, holte man viele Tausend Chinesen ins Land. Es kamen auch Japaner, Filipinos und Indonesier nach Kalifornien. Vor allem in San Francisco bestehen weitausgedehnte, menschenwimmelnde China-Towns.

Das überaus günstige Klima, vor allem die vielen Sonnentage, lockten die Filmschaffenden herbei, schon bald nachdem die Kinematographie erfunden war. Heute hat HOLLYWOOD schon alte Tradition, und viele Meilen weit breiten sich die Studios aus. Der Besuch solcher Anlagen ist durchaus zu empfehlen und jederzeit möglich. Ein Tag allein wird fürs DISNEYLAND bei Los Angeles kaum genügen. Der einstmals größte und feinste Ozeanriese der sieben Weltmeere, die „Queen MARY", wurde zum schwimmenden Museum. Sie liegt bei Los Angeles, und wer will, kann dort nicht nur essen, sondern auch wohnen. Fremde Touristen wie auch die Kalifornier kommen aus dem Staunen nicht heraus, wenn sie die sogenannten „MARINELANDS" von San Diego im Süden bis hinauf über San Francisco besuchen. Da schweben blonde Mädchen auf dem Rücken von Schwertwalen (Killerwhales) übers Wasser, und sogar Walfische erfreuen die Besucher mit Kunststücken. Im Zoo von San Diego sieht man die einzigen außerhalb von Australien lebenden KOALA-BÄREN. Ebenso erstaunlich sind mehr als hundert PINGUINE verschiedener Art, für die man hinter riesigen Glaswänden ein echt antarktisches Biotop geschaffen hat. Sogar die Lichtverhältnisse entsprechen dem südlichen Eismeer, was die Pinguine erfreulicherweise veranlaßt hat, sich zu paaren, zu brüten und Nachkommen aufzuziehen.

Eines der neuesten und wohl kostbarsten Museen der Welt, das „MALIBU" bei Los Angeles, dürfte einmalig sein. Der weltbekannte Ölmilliardär Paul Getty hat es mit sagenhaften Sammlungen der Allgemeinheit gestiftet. Eintritt frei, aber Anmeldung zu empfehlen.

Überhaupt ist das glückliche, das superreiche Kalifornien mit Museen, Sammlungen und Stiftungen fast aller denkbarer Arten reich gesegnet. Das gilt auch für „SAN SIMEON", seinerzeit geschaffen von dem amerikanischen Pressezaren und Beherrscher der Filmindustrie William Randolph Hearst. Seine phantastische Schöpfung, über der Big-Sur-Traumstraße, nahe dem Camino Real gelegen, besteht aus einer ganzen Sammlung von Schlössern, die mit dem Kunstschaffen aus fast allen Ländern der Welt gefüllt sind. Das alles ist aufgebaut und ausgestellt in einem herrlich weiten, wohlgepflegten Park. Viele Teile der Bauten wurden aus der antiken, der exotischen Welt auf dem Seewege, dann über Land nach San Simeon geschafft, um sie in neugebaute Fassaden einzufügen. Nicht immer geschah das auf geschmackvolle Weise, aber für sich allein betrachtet ist das meiste schon sehenswert und kostbar auf jeden Fall. Sammlungen ganz verschiedener Art innerhalb der Paläste verdienen Bewunderung. Man traut seinen Augen nicht, was der damals unermeßliche Reichtum des William Hearst dank seiner blühenden Phantasie in San Simeon geschaffen hat. Das HUNTINGDON-MUSEUM bei Los Angeles, mit besserem Geschmack eingerichtet, kann möglicherweise San Simeon an Qualität wie Kostbarkeit übertreffen. Der zum Huntingdon-Museum gehörende Park, einige Quadratkilometer ausgedehnt, enthält eine Sammlung von Kakteen, die an Vielfalt der Arten alles sonst auf der Welt übertrifft. So jedenfalls sagt man dort.

Wollte sich der Kalifornienfreund alle Museen anschauen, die man eigentlich sehen sollte, müßte er bald nach Neujahr damit beginnen, um Weihnachten wieder daheim zu sein. Es gibt nämlich auch Museen, die ziemlich versteckt liegen, vor allem solche, die ihre Existenz einem privaten Stifter verdanken. So hatte ich große Mühe, das SÜDWEST-MUSEUM zu finden, aus dessen Namen nicht hervorgeht, daß es sich dabei nur um indianisches Kulturgut handelt.

Nicht versäumen sollte man das Überschreiten einer über 150 Jahre alten Brücke, die sich unmittelbar bei HAVASU-CITY befindet, wo sie einen künstlich geschaffenen Arm des Colorado River überquert. Eingeweiht wurde das aus massivem Granitstein bestehende Bauwerk vom britischen König Wilhelm IV. am 1. Mai 1835. Damals aber spannte es sich über die Themse. Als die LONDON-BRIDGE hundert Jahre später nicht mehr dem Verkehr genügte, hat man sie abgerissen und das gesamte Baumaterial, insgesamt hundertfünfzigtausend Tonnen, an einen geschäftstüchtigen Amerikaner verkauft. Der war im Begriff, im sonnendurchfluteten Grenzgebiet von Kalifornien zu Arizona eine SENIOREN-CITY zu bauen, mitten in einer Halbwüste, wo es nur Dornbüsche und Stachelkakteen gab. Aber spottbillig war das Gelände zu haben. Die sensationelle Verlegung der alten London-Bridge sollte es aufwerten und die Seniorenstadt bekannt machen. Weil für die Brücke kein Wasserlauf vorhanden war, mußte man ihn erst anlegen. Die Nähe des Colorado-River machte es möglich. Fünf Millionen Dollar verschlang das werbewirksame Unternehmen, und so spannt sich nun die alte London-Bridge über den Havasu-Creek.

An der Küste hinauf und hinab, wo immer sich Buchten öffnen oder Wellenbrecher ins Meer gebaut wurden, liegen unzählige Segelboote und Motoryachten. Es gibt sie in jeder Art und Größe, äußerst einfach und zweckmäßig gebaut bis zum ganz großen Luxus. An schönen Feiertagen ist das blaugrüne Wasser bis weit hinaus von vielen, sogar allzu vielen Booten bedeckt. Draußen gibt es Inseln und ganze Inselgruppen, wie beispielsweise die CATALINAS, wo seltengewordene Tiere, vor allem aus der Vogelwelt, so gut beschützt werden, daß sie den Menschen gestatten, sich bis auf wenige Meter zu nähern. Es fehlen nicht Badestrände, Tanzlokale, Spielkasinos und die üblichen Scharen von hochgewachsenen, schlanken, braungebrannten Mädchen. Viele haben nur wenig und manche fast gar nichts auf ihrer

glatten Haut. In bestimmten Straßen, meist in den Außenbezirken großer Städte, wie beispielsweise auf dem endlos langen, kurvenreichen SUNSET BOULEVARD von Los Angeles, wimmelt es von Hippies, Punks, Homos und Hermanas und wie sonst die Ausgeflippten genannt werden. Nicht wenige sind von Kopf bis Fuß mit Glitzerketten und anderem Krimskrams behängt, auf den Schultern lebende Erdhörnchen oder niedliche Ratten mit gelben Nagezähnen. Eigentlich sind alle harmlos, die Menschen wie Tiere, sogar ausgesprochen freundlich.

Ganz anders die weltweit berühmten Ferienkolonien der oberen Zehntausend, wie das angeblich superfeine PALMSPRINGS. Dort leben die reichsten und erfolgreichsten Amerikaner im Frühjahr, Herbst und oft auch im Winter. Aber zu sehen sind die nur selten. Ihre gar nicht so üppigen, zumeist ebenerdigen Häuser liegen versteckt in großen Gärten. Bei ihnen herrscht insofern Apartheid, als sie nur miteinander verkehren und Golf spielen in den eigenen Klubs.

Wenn es auch nur wenige feste Punkte und wirkungsvolle Missionen gab im damaligen NEUMEXIKO, ARIZONA, NEVADA, COLORADO und UTAH, war doch auf mittelbare Weise der spanische Einfluß groß und ist es in gewisser Weise bis heute geblieben. Von den Spaniern und Mexikanern stammten fast alle Haustiere, die weitgehend das Leben der Eingeborenen verändert haben. Die Kunst des Silberschmiedens und die Herstellung bunter Wolldecken, wie sie gerade von den Navajos und den Hopis entwickelt wurden, wären ohne die Spanier nicht möglich gewesen.

Ungefähr ein Zehntel von Arizona gehört noch, besser gesagt gehört wieder den Indianern. Die amerikanische Regierung hat schon seit geraumer Zeit den NAVAJO wie auch den HOPI fast völlig die Verwaltung ihrer Reservate überlassen. Viel höher stand schon in alten Zeiten ihre Entwicklung über den noch fast im Naturzustand lebenden Ureinwohnern Kaliforniens. Als seinerzeit die Navajos während der grausamen Indianerkriege und nach der Vertreibung aus ihren Stammesgebieten bis auf knapp siebentausend halbverhungerte Überlebende reduziert waren, hat sich das Volk der Navajos binnen nur hundert Jahren auf fast 200 000 Köpfe vermehrt, und die bewohnen wieder ihre alte Heimat. Weiter noch steigt ihr Geburtenüberschuß von Jahr zu Jahr. Nicht so bei den Hopi, deren Zahl sich im gleichen Zeitraum bestenfalls verdoppelt hat und heute rund dreitausend Menschen beträgt. Das relativ kleine Reservat der Hopi wird ganz vom riesigen Reservat der Navajos eingeschlossen. Dennoch handelt es sich um zwei völlig verschiedene Völkerschaften, mit anderer Sprache und sehr verschiedenem Brauchtum.

Im Canyon de Chelly, das gleichfalls zum Reservat der Navajo gehört, leben während des Sommers ein paar hundert Familien. Viele bewohnen nach wie vor die gleichen Hogans, wie vor Jahrhunderten oder vor Jahrtausenden ihre Vorfahren.

Es sind sechseckige, bisweilen achteckige Hütten aus massiven Stämmen, mit Lehm oder Rasenstücken abgedeckt. In dem endlos langen, von steilen Wänden eingefaßten Chelly Canyon gibt es Höhlen mit sogenannten Cliffdwellings, die während unsicherer Zeiten bewohnt waren. Noch gut erhalten sind bemalte Wände mit rätselhaften Symbolen.

Andere Höhlenburgen sind mehrere hundert Meter breit, sie wurden tief in die Höhlen senkrechter Wände eingebaut. Man findet sie in den Schluchten der bis zu 2500 Meter aufsteigenden Mesas. Ein spanisches Wort, das „Tisch" bedeutet und Berge wie Gebirge bezeichnet, die oben flach sind, aber getrennt durch tiefe, steile Täler. Die Höhlenbewohner alter Zeit lebten von den Feldern, auch wildwachsenden Pflanzen in der Schlucht. Bei Not und Gefahr eilten sie über schmale Leitern hinauf in ihre Höhlen, die leicht zu verteidigen waren. Vorräte waren angehäuft, und kühles Quellwasser gab es auch. Bis zu zweihundertfünfzig gemauerte Räume hat man in einigen der Cliffdwellings gezählt. Nach dem Dia-Karbon-Verfahren konnte man feststellen, daß die Blütezeit der Mesakultur von Anfang des elften bis etwa zur Mitte des vierzehnten Jahrhunderts gedauert hat. Auch hier waren die sagenhaften Anasazi, die „Älten" am Werk. Aber weshalb zur etwa gleichen Zeit die Cliffdwellings verlassen wurden, weiß man nicht.

Ein großer Teil der Naturwunder im amerikanischen Südwesten liegt im Monument Valley. Die Bilder in diesem Band beweisen es. Ursprünglich war alles ein rund 1500 Meter hohes Felsenplateau. Im Verlauf von Jahrmillionen haben Wasser, Eis und Schneeschmelze zum größten Teil das Gelände abgetragen, aber die aus festem Stein bestehende Schicht lediglich zernagt. Da stehen nun in bizarrer Form die Reste als hoch aufragende Türme und riesige Höhlentore. Man fällt von einem Staunen ins andere, hat am Ende aber doch nur einen kleinen Teil der Wunderwerke vor Augen gehabt.

Auch im Staat Utah gibt es eine Fülle von Wunderwerken der Natur, die man glücklicherweise beizeiten unter Staatsschutz gestellt hat. Dazu gehören in verblüffend großer Zahl die NATÜRLICHEN BRÜCKEN. Allein im Schutzgebiet „ARCHES NATIONALPARK" sind 89 solcher Brücken vorhanden. Das Wasser hat sie während undenklich langer Zeit ausgewaschen, und sie spannen sich nun über Abgründe bis zu fünfzig Meter breit und fünfzig Meter tief. Manche sind droben nur so schmal und dünn, daß man kaum wagt hinüberzugehen. Aber wer mutig ist, tut es sogar zu Pferde.

Ein unglaubliches Gebilde über das andere haben die Kräfte der Natur in vielen Jahrmillionen geschaffen und noch lange nicht damit aufgehört. Das BRYCE-CANYON im Südosten von Utah ist gleichfalls eine Naturschöpfung, die sich mit nichts anderem vergleichen läßt. Aus menschenleerer Wildnis erheben sich seine vielzackigen, beim Aufgang wie beim Untergang der Sonne rotglühenden Steintürme. Trotz aller Unzugänglichkeit haben schon 1776 spanische Patres den Bryce-Canyon entdeckt und vor seiner Wildheit gewarnt. Amerikanische Pelzhändler kamen im Jahr 1821 dorthin, und die MORMONEN aus Utah gründeten 1864 dort ihre Siedlungen.

Wie jeder weiß, ist die größte, die allergrößte Sehenswürdigkeit des amerikanischen Südwestens der GRAND CANYON, eine bis zu 1600 Meter tiefe Schlucht des Colorado River. Schon im Jahre 1542 wurde dieses Wunder der Welt von LOPE DE CARDENAS entdeckt, der zur Expedition des Francisco Coronado gehörte. Auch die besten Fotos können nicht wiedergeben, wie bei Sonnenaufgang und -untergang die rasch wechselnde Beleuchtung wirkt.

Vielleicht noch sehenswerter ist meines Erachtens das weit weniger bekannte HAVASU-TAL. Drunten in der schmalen, nicht gar so langen, von üppiger Vegetation erfüllten Schlucht leben die HAVASUPAI-INDIANER, deren Name sich am ehesten mit „Grünwassermenschen" übersetzen läßt. Sie haben dort ihr Reservat, und nur wenn sie es erlauben, dürfen in begrenzter Zahl Besucher hinein. Der Abstieg, falls gestattet, geschieht am besten auf Maultieren, wobei zu beachten ist, daß nicht der geringste Abfall drunten bleiben darf.

Da will ich am letzten Tag meines Aufenthalts von BORREGO SPRINGS nach Los Angeles fliegen, um von dort über die Frankfurter Drehscheibe mein liebes München zu erreichen. Ein Luftsprung nur von Borrego nach LA. Die erwartete nur achtsitzige Cessna reicht dafür aus. Aber die kommt nicht, obwohl alle paar Minuten ihre Ankunft gemeldet wird. Nur ein Angestellter betreut den Miniflugplatz von Borrego und gibt an, daß wieder dichter Nebel die ausbleibende Maschine auf Abwege drängt. Da ist noch ein Flugreisender, der ebenso ungeduldig wartet.

„Immer wieder erleb' ich das in diesem Land", schimpft der hochgewachsene, schon ältere Mann mit auffallend energischem Gesicht. Mißmutig sieht er dabei aus, doch seine Augen verraten Energie.

„Leichter fliegt man auf den Mond als von hier nach „LOS ANGELES", flucht der Wartegenosse, „da geht's pünktlich los und genau auf die Minute ist man droben." Gerade wollte ich lachen über den blöden Scherz, aber der Mann hinter dem Schalter warnte mich.

„Scherz beiseite, der Gentleman meint's ernst", sagte er mir, „Sie reden mit Neil Armstrong, dem ersten Mann auf dem Mond . . . am 21. Juli 1969 ist das gewesen."

La Californie merveilleuse

On ne s'arrête pas à l'Etat qui porte ce nom quand on dit Californie aux Etats-Unis. La notion Californie a dépassé les frontières et englobe tout ce que les Espagnols ont découvert, exploré ou même seulement effleuré en leur temps. N'oublions pas que jusqu'en 1848, la région entière appartenait encore au Mexique, du moins sur le papier.

Les régions entourant la Californie partagent avec celle-ci des structures climatiques, géologiques et géographiques. Il apparaît donc justifiable de les inclure dans cet ouvrage sans s'en tenir au tracé de la carte de l'Etat.

La Californie offre à l'homme tout ce qu'il peut désirer sur la terre. Un climat tempéré, des sols fertiles et un ensoleillement de deux cent cinquante jours en moyenne par an. Les plages de sable fin alternent avec les côtes d'un romantisme sauvage. Montagnes recouvertes de neige, forêts d'un vert profond, vallées d'une beauté inouïe, paysages multiples de la Californie. De vastes plateaux balayés par les vents qui se transforment soudain en mers de fleurs; steppes d'arbustes épineux qui s'étendent à perte de vue, forêts de cactées et de plantes grasses, oasis de palmiers où jaillissent des sources fraîches, lacs enchanteurs aux formes et coloris variés, souvent nichés dans des montagnes recouvertes, selon l'altitude, de neiges éternelles. Tous ces spectacles somptueux de la nature existent en Californie. Le troisième Etat des USA s'étend le long de l'Océan Pacifique, sur plus de 1250 kilomètres et sur plus de dix degrés de longitude. De la mer à ses frontières, sa largeur mesure de 230 à 1000 kilomètres. Cet immense territoire a une superficie de 411 000 kilomètres alors que la République fédérale d'Allemagne n'en compte que 249 000. Mais tandis que 60 millions d'habitants vivent en RFA, la Californie, pays bien plus vaste, n'en totalise que 22 millions. Cette population augmente toutefois au fil des années en raison d'une immigration importante à partir des autres Etats américains et (souvent illégale celle-ci) en provenance du Mexique.

Le paysage de la Californie et des contrées avoisinantes est aussi varié que le climat. On passe des déserts les plus brûlants aux neiges éternelles sans compter les deux mille kilomètres de côtes du Pacifique. Il faut donc tenir compte des variations et surtout ne pas se fier aux bulletins météorologiques. Un soleil de plomb tapera sur la Vallée de la Mort alors qu'une tourmente de neige bloquera l'entrée du Parc de Sequoia. La Californie est le pays des superlatifs. C'est là en effet que se dresse la plus haute montagne des Etats-Unis (Alaska non compris), le Mont Whitney, avec ses 4418 mètres. C'est là également que se trouve le point le plus bas de tout le continent – environ 90 mètres sous le niveau de la mer – près de Badswater, dans la Vallée de la Mort. Cette vallée de 7700 kilomètres carrés, brûlante et désertique, compte parmi les sites protégés de Californie. Ils sont appelés «Parcs» et «Parcs nationaux», mais ne ressemblent en rien à des espaces entretenus par la main des hommes. Au contraire, ils sont laissés autant que possible dans leur état sauvage et naturel. Le touriste qui cherche à visiter tous les superlatifs de la Californie aura fort à faire. Les contrastes sont extrêmement marqués dans le pays. On peut y voir les plus grands et les plus vieux arbres du monde. Le Methusala Park est riche en conifères «pinus aristatus», de petits arbres qui existaient déjà à l'époque où le pharaon Cheops entamait la construction de sa pyramide.

La Californie possède des volcans en activité et d'autres qui entrent en éruption de temps à autre et dévastent des régions entières comme récemment le Mount Helen, dans l'Etat de Washington. Les tremblements de terre n'épargnent pas non plus la région. Une secousse sismique suivie d'incendies a ainsi détruit San Francisco, il y a quatre-vingts ans de cela.

Un nombre infini de plantes croît en Californie. Les diverses sortes de fruits tropicaux, introduits au 18ème siècle par les missionnaires espagnols se sont développées à profusion. Il faut dire que la Californie offre, dans de nombreuses régions, les sols et climats idéaux. Tout ce que les pionniers ont apporté de la vieille Europe et des coins les plus reculés de la terre a littéralement prospéré en Californie. Que ce soit les animaux domestiques inconnus jusque là en Amérique comme les moutons, les chèvres, les bovins, les chevaux et les ânes ainsi que toutes les espèces possibles et imaginables de volaille. Les dindons en revanche existaient déjà: ce sont eux qui nous sont venus d'Amérique centrale.

Les richesses de la région: l'or, l'argent, le cuivre, le pétrole et autres matières premières très recherchées, sont loin d'être taries. Un réseau de routes excellentes quadrille le pays. La vitesse est toutefois limitée à 60 miles (96 km/h) sur les autoroutes à cinq ou même six chaussées.

La plus belle route de la Californie, appelée la voie de rêve du monde, la nationale I est mieux connue sous le nom de BIG SUR. Un tronçon de cette route, incomparable, longe la côte de Monterey à la baie de Morro. La précaution est de rigueur sur cette route sinueuse qui grimpe et descend entre des amas de roches. Mais le chauffeur, condamné au luxe de la lenteur, voit à chaque tournant, surgir un tableau d'une beauté sauvage. C'est un kaléidoscope de rochers déchiquetés et de couleurs, de déferlements majestueux de flots, de vagues mourant doucement sur les grèves, de champs de varech bercés par la mer. Des îles, hautes et abruptes comme des tours d'église, se dressent au dessus des flots et des criques profondes rappellent les fjords norvégiens. La région du BIG SUR est certainement l'endroit le plus désert de la Californie. Il n'était habité que de quelques centaines de nomades primitifs quand en 1770, le père franciscain Junipero Serra fonda la mission du Carmel sur la baie de St. Lucia.

Le CHAPPARAL recouvre toujours les montagnes qui surplombent la route du Big Sur. Aucun colon n'est venu s'installer dans ce désert de buissons épineux depuis une éternité. Les moutons ou les boeufs n'y trouveraient pas de pâturages et le sol en est incultivable. Le premier colon, apparu aux alentours de 1880, un Allemand du nom de Pfeifer, réussit pourtant à se bâtir une existence sur cette terre aride. C'est pourtant à sa nombreuse descendance et à ses voisins très actifs que l'on doit l'exploitation de la contrée. Les Pfeifers ont laissé leur nom à une multitude de communes, montagnes et cours d'eau de la région. Par la suite, celui qui oeuvra le plus fut sans aucun doute William Randolph Hearst. Son domaine SAN SIMEON s'étend de la côte jusqu'à l'intérieur des montagnes. C'est un admirable ensemble de châteaux, de musées et de parcs qui auraient coûté plus de 1000 millions de dollars au roi de la presse et maître de Hollywood.
Tout le long du trajet, le touriste peut s'arrêter sur des parkings créés aux endroits qui offrent les vues les plus admirables: sur des pointes de terre s'avançant sur la mer. Armé d'un peu de patience et de bonnes jumelles, il verra des otaries, des phoques et même des éléphants de mer évoluer sur la plage. Au large, il découvrira peut-être des cachalots, des baleines grises et qui sait? La baleine bleue, le plus grand animal terrestre. Inoubliable, le spectacle des loutres de mer! A la fin du siècle dernier, on avait cru décimés à jamais ces animaux superbes et inoffensifs, chassés sans pitié durant des années pour leur fourrure précieuse. Mais miracle, quelques-uns réapparurent en 1937. Aujourd'hui, protégées et surveillées, les loutres de mer se sont multipliées jusqu'à une centaine de milliers.
La population californienne a connu une évolution rapide, surtout en ce qui concerne les immigrés venus des autres Etats américains et d'Europe. Les Californiens présentent une belle apparence; ils sont en général hauts de stature et respirent la santé et la fraîcheur. Ils sont toutefois imbus de leur supériorité et tournent un regard des plus optimiste vers l'avenir. Que l'on ne se risque surtout pas à critiquer le pays ou ses habitants! Ils ne le supporteraient pas. La Californie, trente et unième Etat des Etats-Unis et le plus peuplé, représente la plus grande merveille du monde pour ses habitants!
La Californie à elle seule comprend quatre parcs nationaux remarquablement entretenus. Des lois spéciales protègent 18 autres sites de la décadence et la destruction. Les touristes arrivant d'une Europe surpeuplée et étranglée par les constructions ne peuvent qu'être stupéfaits des efforts efficaces que les Californiens entreprennent depuis des années pour sauvegarder leur environnement.

L'histoire du Sud-Ouest des Etats-Unis

Tout a commencé avec les Espagnols, bien qu'au début, un nombre infime d'entre eux seulement n'aient quitté le Mexique pour s'aventurer vers le nord-ouest. Pourtant, leur style architectural et celui de leurs jardins, les plantes et animaux domestiques qu'ils ont apportés, dominent encore dans la région. De nos jours, les sentiers de mulets des missionnaires suivent quelques-unes des autoroutes modernes et des villes peuplées de plusieurs millions d'habitants se dressent sur l'emplacement des anciennes missions. C'est pourquoi ces agglomérations actuelles portent toutes des noms espagnols: ceux des saints de l'Eglise catholique.

HERNANDO CORTEZ, conquérant et vice-roi du Mexique, découvrit la Californie vers l'an 1535 et en explora même la partie sud. Cette région n'était toutefois pas la Californie américaine, mais la basse Californie, appartenant encore aujourd'hui au Mexique. C'est l'étroite péninsule, de Baja California longue de quelque mille kilomètres. La tentative espagnole de coloniser si tôt cette terre lointaine se termina toutefois par un échec. En revanche, des marins audacieux explorèrent la côte, poussèrent jusqu'au Canada et atteignirent même l'Alaska. Le premier Européen à pénétrer la Californie actuelle fut sans doute HERNANDO DE ALARCON. Les Espagnols ne s'avancèrent toutefois pas à l'intérieur du pays. Leur empire avait déjà pris des proportions immenses et la mère patrie ne possédait plus assez d'effectifs pour s'implanter dans de nouvelles régions. Ils se contentèrent de la BAIE DE MONTEREY bien abritée des tempêtes. Elle leur servait de station intermédiaire où la flotte de commerce venait mouiller deux fois par an en cours de trajet, entre le port D'ACAPULCO sur la côte ouest du Mexique et MANILA, la capitale des Philippines espagnoles. A cette époque, on parlait de la Californie en employant le pluriel: LAS CALIFORNIAS. C'était une région immense qui descendait le long de la côte jusqu'à la péninsule inexplorée de Baja California et remontait vers le nord, aussi loin qu'un navire espagnol ait jamais navigué. Les Espagnols étaient persuadés que tous ces territoires appartenaient à la couronne d'Espagne!
C'est en 1700 que commencèrent l'exploration et le développement systématiques de la Californie. La première mission nommée LA PAZ fut fondée en 1691 à la pointe sud de la basse Californie. SAN SOLENO, la dernière fut bâtie en 1822 au nord de la baie de San Francisco. Les 31 missions, celles de Baja California incluses, formaient une chaîne de quelque 2000 kilomètres à vol d'oiseau. Une oeuvre admirable sinon gigantesque pour l'époque! La Californie américaine actuelle abritait 21 missions reliées par une route, le «Camino Real» (la voie royale). On ne pouvait emprunter cette piste qu'avec des charrettes cahotantes, à dos de cheval ou encore de mulet. Mais on y rencontrait surtout des voyageurs à pied presque toujours chargés de lourds fardeaux.

Presque toutes les missions de la basse Californie, la Baja California, sont tombées en ruine au cours des cinquante dernières années. Il ne reste plus que quelques traces du «Camino Real», la voie royale. J'ai tenté sans succès d'en suivre au moins deux ou trois kilomètres ... Par contre, dans l'Etat américain de Californie, toutes les missions ont été conservées ou reconstituées. Sans retrouver toutes leur figure ancienne, elles ont pourtant été si bien restaurées que se dégage d'elles l'atmosphère d'autrefois. On peut encore voir de nombreuses parties de l'agencement original et visiter par exemple la chambre d'hôte qui était réservée aux officiers et envoyés du gouvernement. Il existe des églises et des chapelles renfermant des autels où prêcha le père Junipero Serra, fondateur des premières missions. Les installations préservées permettent aux visiteurs de se faire une image précise de la vie des missions et des fonctions diverses que chacune avait à remplir. Elles ne travaillaient pas seulement à sauver de l'enfer les âmes païennes des Indiens. Il s'agissait aussi de coloniser ceux-ci, d'améliorer leurs structures sociales et de les aider à progresser vers la civilisation. Les premiers habitants de la Californie, très primitifs, se sustentaient à grand-peine et étaient désarmés devant des ennemis comme les animaux sauvages. On ne peut donc les comparer aux Mayas et aux Aztèques du Mexique pas plus qu'aux Indiens Pueblos ou aux habitants des Mesas. Six, sept, huit peuples traversèrent la région à cette époque, chacun possédant des mœurs et langues différents. Les rapports laissés par les missionnaires décrivent ces tribut comme étant craintives, timides et ensuite dociles. Elles se rendaient volontairement chez les frères et les pères catholiques. Les missions les protégeaient de leurs ennemis, leur donnaient un toit et les nourrissaient. Les niveaux d'intelligence et de bonne volonté des autochtones variaient fort. Ils se révélaient dans les tâches attribuées et les capacités d'assimiler de nouvelles connaissances. Certains Indiens devinrent forgerons, potiers ou tisserands. Plusieurs apprirent même l'art de l'écriture, de la lecture et du calcul. D'autres ne purent jamais qu'accomplir les besognes les plus simples. Quelques tribus résistèrent pourtant à toute tentative de conversion. Elles attaquaient parfois les missions et exterminaient les Franciscains sans défense. Des PRESIDIOS comprenant une douzaine de soldats espagnols menés par un officier furent alors attachés à chaque fondation religieuse aux fins d'en protéger les résidents. Mais des difficultés opposaient souvent les moines aux militaires. Les soldats, rudes et jeunes pour la plupart, s'enivraient du vin que les missionnaires produisaient pour la messe, poursuivaient les femmes et donnaient en général un très mauvais exemple aux enfants indiens baptisés. Afin de sauvegarder la vertu de leurs ouailles, les pieux Franciscains exigèrent que les Presidios et les habitations des colons soient éloignés de quelques miles des missions. Mais les soldats arrivaient souvent trop tard quand l'une d'entre elles était

attaquée. L'ordre des Franciscains parvint finalement à coloniser la plupart des autochtones. Les éducateurs religieux ne se fiaient pourtant pas entièrement à la bonne moralité de leurs ouailles. Au coucher du soleil, ils enfermaient à clé toutes les jeunes filles et les femmes dont les maris étaient absents! Quelques Indiens baptisés développèrent de véritables talents artistiques. On peut encore admirer aujourd'hui dans de nombreuses missions des œuvres peintes et sculptées révélant un art indien très particulier. Les fondations des missionnaires pratiquaient l'autosuffisance. On y fabriquait ce qui était nécessaire à la vie quotidienne. Par la suite, les missions exportèrent même vers le Mexique ou vers la mère patrie certains produits tels le savon, le cuir tanné, la chandelle et la poudre d'os. Le visiteur d'une mission rénovée sera stupéfait à la vue des nombreux ateliers et instruments agricoles, témoins des structures homogènes établies par les moines.

SAN DIEGO, proche de la frontière du Mexique, devint en 1769, la première mission de l'ordre des Franciscains dans l'actuelle Californie américaine. Le capitaine Gaspar de Portala qui arrivait du Mexique la rejoignit, accompagné, mené plutôt par l'infatigable père Junipero Serra. Ce moine avait été le premier à explorer les voies d'accès au cours de longues et pénibles marches dans des régions alors inconnues. Deux-cent-vingts colons dont des femmes et des enfants suivaient les soldats et les missionnaires à pied. Ils apportaient avec eux de nombreuses espèces d'animaux domestiques, des semences et des ustensiles indispensables. Comme on escomptait la perte d'une grande partie du groupe, sa disparition totale même, trois navires supplémentaires voguèrent vers l'Amérique avec à leur bord d'autres contingents de soldats, missionnaires et colons. Tandis qu'un tiers du premier groupe périssait en cours de route sur le sol californien, deux des trois vaisseaux atteignaient la baie de San Diego. La soif, la faim, la maladie avaient décimé plus de la moitié des équipages et voyageurs durant la traversée.

La mission de San Diego était à peine établie que l'exploration dans l'inconnu se poursuivit. Soldats et pionniers, conduits par le père Serra, s'avancèrent péniblement vers le nord, à travers des masses de rochers, des steppes de buissons épineux et des cols de montagne dangereux. Derrière eux, grinçaient et bringuebalaient les charrettes à bœufs. Environ à la même période, deux vaisseaux tentaient d'atteindre le même objectif qui avait été convenu d'avance. De lourdes pertes humaines accompagnaient toujours les progressions à l'intérieur des territoires étrangers, mais elles faisaient partie des aléas et une douzaine d'hommes parvenaient quand même au but. C'est ainsi que furent créées les missions et les stations de CARLOS BORROMEO, DE CARMELO et SAN ANTONIO DE PADUA, de LUIS OBISPO, de SAN JUAN CAPSTRANO, de SANTA CLARA et de SANTA BARBARA pour n'en citer que quelques-unes. SAN GABRIEL ARCANGEL fut fondée en 1771. Aujourd'hui, il faut un plan détaillé de Los Angeles pour découvrir cette ancienne mission restaurée des Franciscains, cachée dans la mer d'édifices de la ville de sept millions d'habitants. Les familles de pionniers et les soldats s'installèrent sur les territoires que le père Serra et le capitaine leur avaient adjugés à plusieurs kilomètres de distance de San Gabriel. L'évangélisation des Franciscains ne devait pas être troublée par la vie d'iniquité du Presidio. Los Angeles dont la largeur atteint parfois 100 kilomètres, possède toujours son noyau d'origine.

On le retrouve à l'angle de style espagnol de la RUE OLVERA et à la PLAZA DE ARMAS, ancien champ d'exercices des soldats du roi d'Espagne. Il reste également une église datant de cette époque. San Gabriel et la rue Olvera, bâties autrefois dans une contrée déserte se fondent à présent dans l'immense agglomération qu'est la troisième ville des Etats-Unis.

Sur les exigences du gouvernement espagnol, les missions et presidios continuèrent de s'étendre vers le nord. Des trappeurs russes venant de Sibérie avaient en effet traversé la mer de Béring pour aller s'installer en ALASKA. Ils avaient fondé des bases dans la partie extrême nord de l'Amérique, sur les îles de Kodiak et de ALEUTEN et faisaient un commerce prospère de peaux de loutres de mer, très recherchées et très chères, avec les Indiens et Esquimos des alentours. Les Espagnols craignaient que les Russes, attirés par des températures plus clémentes, ne s'aventurent vers le sud. Ils ne pouvaient pratiquer ni agriculture ni élevage en Alaska et nécessitaient des sols fertiles pour subvenir à leurs besoins alimentaires. Outre les Russes, un autre danger menaçait également les conquérants espagnols. En été 1792, le rude écossais Alexander Mackenzie était parvenu à traverser le continent américain d'est en ouest. Il avait atteint l'océan Pacifique près de Bellacola, une agglomération située aujourd'hui dans le Canada actuel. Pourquoi les Britanniques ne décideraient-ils pas de descendre la côte jusqu'à la Californie espagnole? Les vassaux du roi d'Espagne devaient absolument devancer cette grave menace. C'est ainsi que d'autres missions furent créées en l'espace de quelques années: SAN JOSÉ en 1796, SAN MIGUEL et SAN JUAN en 1787, deux autres dans les années qui suivirent et la dernière de la chaîne, SAN SOLANO en 1822.

Les missions étaient situées de façon à ce qu'une journée de voyage sépare chacune d'elle. Les distances étaient calculées en fonction des heures de trajet et non pas d'après le nombre de kilomètres. Une piste menait au point d'ancrage le plus proche quand une mission ne se trouvait pas au bord de la mer. De longs mois pouvaient toutefois s'écouler avant qu'un vaisseau ne vienne mouiller. Il fallait donc savoir patienter avant de recevoir les commandes ou les réponses au courrier qu'on

avait envoyés en Espagne. Des périodes de deux années d'attente n'étaient pas rares. Mais la persévérance était souvent récompensée et les descendants des colons espagnols jouissent encore de ses fruits jusqu'à nos jours.

Les rois d'Espagne prétendaient en effet avoir le droit de distribuer des territoires en Californie. Ils gratifiaient ainsi les solliciteurs qui avaient rendu des services ou tout simplement ceux qui promettaient d'accomplir quelque action en faveur de la monarchie. Les limites des futures propriétés n'étaient pas déterminées. La description d'une chaîne de collines ou du cours d'un fleuve suffisait à en contruire les frontières souhaitées. La présence des autochtones sur les terres ne jouait aucun rôle. Du moment qu'un autre candidat ne revendiquait pas le même endroit, le futur propriétaire était certain d'obtenir gain de cause. Il lui fallait toutefois se rendre lui-même en Espagne et présenter personnellement sa requête au roi. C'est ainsi, qu'au début de la colonisation, furent créés ces immenses domaines souvent plus vastes que les duchés de la vieille Europe. L'ÉPOQUE DORÉE DES DONS commençait.

Quelques-uns des nouveaux maîtres ne songèrent même pas à délimiter les frontières de leurs territoires. Leurs troupeaux de bœufs, moutons, chevaux et ânes se multipliaient à l'infini sur des sols fertiles. Les Dons recrutaient leur personnel parmi les milliers d'Indiens baptisés qui résidaient dans les missions. Bien nourrie et vivant au sein d'un environnement protégé, la population indienne s'était tellement accrue que les pères manquaient de place et de travail pour entretenir toute la communauté. Les Indiens ne subirent pas d'exploitation à cette époque. Ils représentaient certes une main-d'œuvre bon marché, mais n'avaient pas à souffrir de la faim. Les produits alimentaires abondaient et même les familles les plus pauvres possédaient des chevaux, des ânes ou des mulets. Les Dons fermaient aussi les yeux si d'aucuns s'appropriaient soit un veau ou un mouton de leurs troupeaux pour se sustenter.

Ce qui aujourd'hui fait partie de la vie quotidienne faisait pourtant défaut. Dans toute la Californie, on ne trouvait ni école, ni enseignants, ni médecins ou dentistes et encore moins d'hôpitaux. Les missionnaires étaient les seuls à s'occuper, dans la mesure de leurs moyens, des malades et des agonisants. Un livre était une rareté et de bons vêtements valaient une fortune. Tout ce que les Dons et les pionniers nécessitaient dans leur vie journalière devait être fabriqué sur place. Les vignobles des missions produisaient du vin à profusion, mais on manquait de verres ou de gobelets pour le boire! Il fallait les importer du Mexique et même d'Espagne. Si d'une part, la Californie de l'époque vivait dans l'abondance, sinon dans le luxe, elle souffrait aussi d'une pénurie des choses les plus courantes de notre existence actuelle.

Les véritables dangers du début du dix-neuvième siècle ne surgirent pas du nord. Les Espagnols n'avaient aucune raison de craindre les immigrés russes installés en Alaska. Sans prendre la peine de consulter Madrid ou le Mexique, DON ANTONIO ARGUELLO, gouverneur espagnol de San Francisco signa en 1805 un accord avec ALEXANDER BARANOW, gouverneur impérial de la Russie en Alaska. L'aristocrate espagnol abandonnait quelques milliers d'hectares de bonne terre aux Russes qui purent y pratiquer culture et élevages de bestiaux et de volailles pour nourrir les trappeurs résidant dans l'Alaska inculte. Les vassaux du Tsar n'en désiraient pas plus et se contentèrent de construire une place fortifiée, FORT ROSS, qui n'abritait qu'une garnison de soixante soldats sibériens. Ils déplacèrent également quelque cent-cinquante indigènes de l'île Aleuten sur la côte californienne car ceux-ci excellaient dans la capture des loutres de mer très prisées.

Les Britanniques ne songeaient pas non plus à venir troubler la vie paisible californienne et le travail efficace des missionnaires. Les comptoirs commerciaux qu'ils avaient fondés à l'embouchure du fleuve Columbia leur suffisaient amplement. Le danger survint d'un pays du sud, du Mexique et entraîna une modification radicale de la Californie. Affaiblie par les harcèlements de Napoléon, l'Espagne n'était plus capable de maîtriser son immense empire colonial. Par ailleurs, la majorité des colonies espagnoles réclamaient leur indépendance. Une rebellion éclata dans la vice-royauté du Mexique contre le vice-roi espagnol qui ne possédait plus le soutien de toutes ses troupes. Une insurrection était à peine écrasée qu'une nouvelle se fomentait et cela durant les vingt années que dura la guerre civile avant que le Mexique n'acquière son autonomie.

Ces événements dramatiques touchèrent à peine la province de la Californie. Au contraire, les gouverneurs de Monterey, San Francisco et Sacramento s'étaient adjugé des status d'indépendance. Malgré leur nombre réduit, les Espagnols se gouvernaient plus ou moins eux-mêmes. Les missions purent donc tout d'abord poursuivre leur œuvre et la chaîne s'étendit bientôt jusqu'à Solano.

La Californie, longtemps isolée du monde extérieur, jouissait d'une existence paisible. Le Mexique possédait à présent son autonomie. Un certain AUGUSTIN D'ITUR-BIDE y avait même été proclamé empereur de 1822 à 1823. Un beau jour, les dirigeants mexicains se rappelèrent pourtant la province californienne. Ils y envoyèrent des gouverneurs armés de nouvelles lois qui obligeaient les Franciscains à céder les missions aux résidents Indiens. Privés des structures anciennes et de l'aide des pères, les indigènes furent incapables de poursuivre l'exploitation des missions. Les Franciscains, quelques Dons et même des gouverneurs mexicains tentèrent aussi longtemps qu'ils le purent de sauvegarder les missions et le mode de vie

qu'ils avaient établi. Mais en 1834, seize des vingt-et-une missions n'existaient déjà plus. Aucune ne fonctionnait cinq années plus tard. Des représentants corrompus du gouvernement mexicain se les étaient appropriées ou les avaient distribuées à leur entourage. Les missions furent aussi livrées au pillage, l'on arracha jusqu'aux tuiles fabriquées par les Indiens pour les utiliser à d'autres fins. De nombreuses églises se retrouvèrent transformées en hangars. Des maladies introduites dans la région décimèrent les Indiens abandonnés à leur sort et n'épargnèrent pas non plus ceux vivant dans la nature sauvage. Aujourd'hui, il ne reste plus qu'un nombre infime de membres de ces tribus.

La rareté des contrôles frontaliers permettait à n'importe qui de pénétrer dans la province californienne. Des trappeurs et pionniers, suivis ou accompagnés d'aventuriers, d'escrocs et de bandes de hors-la-loi, avaient atteint l'Ouest sauvage. Après avoir traversé l'immensité de la prairie, ils étaient parvenus aux Montagnes Rocheuses, derrière lesquelles s'étendaient les vallées fertiles, les pâturages et les forêts de la Californie. Une belle et riche région qui appartenait à la République du Mexique. Mais on savait qu'une guerre civile permanente régnait chez les Mexicains et qu'une simple poignée d'hommes dirigeaient la province convoitée. Dès 1826, des trappeurs franchirent les Montagnes Rocheuses. Ils posèrent leurs pièges sur l'autre versant et firent du commerce avec les Indiens. Ils surgissaient parfois chez les Dons, souvent impuissants à résister aux intrus. Les agressions, pillages de domaines, voire meurtres de leurs habitants se firent fréquents. Le gouvernement américain protestait quand les coupables étaient arrêtés. Il fallait les relâcher, même si on les avait déjà incarcérés dans des prisons mexicaines. Les aventuriers américains et les immigrés européens tirèrent bientôt profit de ce régime plus que libéral. De longues caravanes de chariots, transportant des familles avides de terres, prirent la direction du Sud. Mais il fallait d'abord franchir les barrages des Indiens et les obstacles des Rocheuses et nombreux furent ceux qui ne virent jamais la terre promise. Pourtant, une fois arrivés sur le versant ensoleillé, les rescapés découvrirent des étendues à perte de vue. Dans les premiers temps, chacun s'emparait des terrains qui lui convenaient, même s'ils étaient déjà la propriété d'un autre. Aucun tribunal ou lois n'existaient pour punir ce genre de vols, sinon celles du plus fort ou du mieux armé.

L'histoire du pays, contée dans les livres d'école américains ne ressemble en rien à celle que rapportent les historiens mexicains ou espagnols. Les Américains étaient persuadés qu'une région renfermant tant de richesses et si peu peuplée de Blancs ne pouvait que leur être destinée. Ils se croyaient seuls capables de développer les immenses possibilités qu'offrait le pays. Ils envoyèrent alors secrètement des agents et éléments perturbateurs qui devaient créer des troubles dans le but de chasser les Mexicains.

Le Texas avait déjà subit le sort qui attendait la Californie. Cette vaste contrée très peu habitée, appartenait également au Mexique. Mais tant d'Américains s'y introduisirent en fraude que leur nombre dépassa bientôt celui des Mexicains et des descendants espagnols. Les «Yankees» se soulevèrent et proclamèrent «la République libre du Texas». Quelques années plus tard, ils demandaient, avec succès, leur admission au sein des Etats-Unis d'Amérique. L'opposition du président mexicain provoqua en 1846 la guerre contre les Etats-Unis que le Mexique, de force inégale, perdit malgré une résistance inouïe. La signature du traité de HIDALGO GUADELUPE obligea le Mexique à céder la moitié de ses provinces aux Etats-Unis. Cela représentait les Etats américains actuels du Nouveau Mexique, de l'Arizona, du Névada, de l'Utah, une partie du Colorado et bien sûr, toute la Californie. L'armée d'occupation américaine avait aidé à établir un gouvernement provisoire en Californie et quand la province demanda par la suite à rejoindre les Etats-Unis, Washington accepta avec générosité cette requête au demeurant prévisible!

La découverte de l'or dans la vallée de Sacramento, peu de temps après la prise de possession américaine, déclencha l'essor fulgurant de la région. La ruée vers l'or amena quelque soixante mille américains à franchir le Cap Horn si redouté ou l'immense Prairie. L'afflux énorme de tous ces émigrants changea la face de la Californie en quelques années.

Et pourtant, infime fut le nombre de ceux qui eurent la chance de trouver de l'or et de s'en servir pour bâtir de réelles fortunes. Les Mexicains, les Espagnols et leurs descendants se virent bientôt acculer à pactiser avec les nouveaux puissants. Les derniers Indiens, réchappés des maladies ou que l'on n'avait pas encore chassés du pays, disparurent à leur tour. La plupart des Dons furent tout simplement dépossédés de leurs terres. La haute société, gardienne de la culture, se vit destituée de ses pouvoirs et sombra dans l'isolation. C'est peut-être pourquoi quelques-unes de ces familles existent encore aujourd'hui. Elles forment un cercle restreint, soucieux de conserver son exclusivité.

A l'heure actuelle, la Californie compte de nouveau une large population de «Latinos». Le nombre des Mexicains qui entrent légalement et le plus souvent illégalement dans le pays, ne cesse d'augmenter. Des inscriptions telles «Amis, go home» (Américains, rentrez chez vous) apparaissent quelquefois sur les murs. Ce rêve des Mexicains ne se réalisera pourtant jamais. Finalement, ce sont les Américains qui ont fait de la Californie ce qu'elle est aujourd'hui.

Après des dizaines d'années de troubles et de tumulte, l'ordre et la loi s'installèrent de nouveau dans la région. L'économie prospéra et est toujours florissante de nos jours. Des villes animées poussèrent sur les lieux des anciennes missions des Franciscains et des Présidios mexicains ou espagnols. SAN FRANCISCO, le cœur de la région, n'en était pourtant pas la capitale. C'est SACRAMENTO, construite après MONTEREY qui devint la ville principale de la Californie. La deuxième moitié du siècle dernier vit une renaissance de l'ordre des Franciscains. En son temps, le président Abraham Lincoln leur avait déjà rendu quelques missions. Les moines reconstruisirent sur les ruines et rétablirent les anciennes structures. Mais un seul des cloîtres, San Luis Rey, put reprendre la fonction primaire de l'ordre qui était de s'occuper des Indiens. Les autres missions devinrent des écoles ou des séminaires pour les prêtres, auxquels des musées sont souvent attachés. Par ailleurs, presque toutes les églises sont de nouveau consacrées au culte.

La guerre civile américaine ne toucha guère la Californie. La province était au contraire une terre d'immigration très prisée et a gardé cette réputation jusqu'à nos jours. Longtemps encore, les longues caravanes de chariots parcoururent les pistes en direction de la terre promise. Et la croissance de la Californie ne connut plus de frontière lorsque le premier chemin de fer traversa tout le continent. Déjà en 1873, des trains directs reliaient New-York à San Francisco. On découvrit des matières premières en masse. Le pétrole jaillit à profusion. Ce fut la naissance et l'expansion de nombreuses industries. La main d'œuvre locale ne suffisant pas, des milliers de Chinois furent amenés dans le pays. Des Japonais, des Philippins et des Indonésiens vinrent grossir et enrichir la population bariolée de la Californie. Témoins en sont les chinatowns regorgeant d'activité des grandes villes et tout particulièrement de San Francisco.

Canyons et Indiens

Le climat et les longues journées d'ensoleillement de la Californie attirèrent les pionniers du cinéma dès les premiers âges de la cinématographie. Les studios D'HOLLYWOOD réputés dans le monde entier représentent une attraction fort intéressante. La visite de DYSNEYLAND, le célèbre parc d'attractions, demanderait plus d'une journée pour le parcourir. Autrefois, le QUEEN MARY, majestueux paquebot de luxe, sillonnait les mers du monde. Il est aujourd'hui ancré à jamais près de Los Angeles et est devenu un musée, un restaurant et un hôtel flottants. Les Californiens partagent l'enthousiasme des touristes étrangers quand ils visitent «MARINELAND», un gigantesque parc aquatique qui remonte de San Diego dans le sud jusqu'à San Francisco. Le visiteur admirera les prouesses artistiques des dauphins et celles des séduisantes dresseuses voltigeant sur le dos de baleines tueuses. Le zoo de San Diego, admirable également, abrite les seuls ours KOALA vivant en dehors de l'Australie. Extraordinaire aussi le spectacle des centaines de PINGOUINS d'espèces variées que l'on voit évoluer dans un immense aquarium. Les conditions biologiques de l'Antarctique y sont exactement reproduites, même celles de la lumière, ce qui permet aux animaux de s'accoupler et de se multiplier à foison. Le milliardaire Paul Getty a rassemblé des collections d'art merveilleuses dans une de ses villas située à MALIBU un des quartiers de Los Angeles. Le roi du pétrole a fait don à la communatué californienne de ce musée unique au monde. La visite en est gratuite, mais il est préférable de s'annoncer à l'avance.
En fait, la Californie regorge de musées, de collections et de fondations des plus variées. L'empereur de la presse et un des maîtres de Hollywood, William Randolph Hearst, fit construire SAN SIMEON au delà du Big Sur, près du Camino Real. Son œuvre fantastique, un ensemble de châteaux riches en œuvres d'art de tous les pays du monde, se dresse au milieu d'un immense parc, admirablement entretenu. De nombreux éléments des édifices ont été importés de la vieille Europe pour être intégrés aux nouvelles façades avec un goût plus ou moins certain. San Simeon vaut toutefois une visite. Les collections à l'intérieur des châteaux sont admirables et l'on reste époustouflé devant l'œuvre née de la fortune démesurée et de l'imagination fertile de William Hearst. Le MUSÉE HUNTINGTON, aux alentours de Los Angeles, merveilleusement bien aménagé, surpasse peut-être San Simeon en qualité et objets précieux. Le parc de quelques kilomètres carrés qui l'entoure comprend une collection de cactées qui serait unique au monde.
Un amateur d'arts, désireux de visiter tous les musées de Californie, devrait remplir un programme qui commencerait le premier jour de l'an pour s'achever à Noël. Il existe de nombreux musées intéressants, mais difficiles à atteindre, surtout ceux qui ont été créés par des donateurs privés. J'ai eu beaucoup de peine à découvrir le musée du SUD-OUEST où l'on peut admirer une très belle collection d'art indien.

Il ne faut surtout pas manquer de franchir un pont vieux de plus de cent-cinquante ans, situé près de HAVASU-CITY. Cette construction massive en pierre de granit, aujourd'hui jetée sur un bras artificiel du fleuve Colorado, fut inaugurée le 1er mai 1835 par le roi britannique Guillaume IV. Mais le pont traversait la Tamise à cette époque. Cent ans plus tard, on démolissait le pont, inapte à supporter la circulation moderne, et ses cent-cinquante mille tonnes de matériaux étaient vendues à un homme d'affaires américain. L'habile commerçant était sur le point de créer une ville pour retraités dans la région baignée de soleil entre la Californie et l'Arizona. Il avait acheté pour une bouchée de pain cette étendue semi-désertique où ne poussaient que des buissons et cactées épineux. La transposition du London Bridge devait accroître la valeur de la région et faire connaître la ville future. Le site ne possédait pas de cours d'eau mais la proximité du Colorado permit d'en créer un. L'entreprise publicitaire dévora cinq millions de dollars et aujourd'hui, le vieux pont de Londres s'élève fièrement au-dessus de la crique de Havasu.

D'innombrables voiliers et yachts sont amarrés le long de la côte, à l'intérieur des criques et là où des brises-lames ont été construits sur la mer. On peut voir des bateaux de toutes sortes et toutes grandeurs, des plus modestes embarcations aux yachts luxueux des milliardaires. Par les beaux jours de fête, ils recouvrent l'eau turquoise jusqu'à l'infini et c'est dommage parfois. Au large, des îles et groupes d'îles comme les CATALINAS abritent des espèces d'animaux devenues rares, surtout appartenant au monde des oiseaux. Ils sont si peu farouches qu'ils permettent aux touristes de les approcher de très près. Les plages, dancings et casinos pullulent, sans oublier la foule de beautés bronzées et sveltes, plus ou moins dénudées. Certaines rues, situées pour la plupart dans les quartiers extérieurs, comme l'interminable SUNSET BOULEVARD de Los Angeles, grouillent de hippies, punkers, homosexuels et autres membres de groupes plus ou moins marginaux. Ils offrent une image colorée, certains ornés de chaînes ou autres décorations de la tête aux pieds, d'autres promenant sur leurs épaules des écureuils domestiqués ou de mignons petits rats aux incisives jaunes. En fait, humains et animaux sont non seulement inoffensifs, mais bien souvent très aimables.
Les colonies de la haute-volée réputées dans le monde entier, tel le soi-disant raffiné PALM SPRING, offrent un aspect totalement contraire. C'est là que les milliardaires américains viennent passer le printemps, l'automne et souvent l'hiver. Mais ils ne se montrent guère. Leurs demeures, des bungalows pour la plupart, se cachent dans des jardins impénétrables. La haute société américain pratique une sorte d'apartheid: elle ne se mélange pas au commun des mortels et ne joue au golf que dans ses propres clubs très fermés.

Le NOUVEAU MEXIQUE, l'ARIZONA, le NÉVADA, l'UTAH et le COLORADO de l'époque ne comptaient que quelques missions et stations. L'influence espagnole s'y fit pourtant fortement sentir et a été conservée jusque nos jours. Les animaux domestiques, par exemple, provenant pour la plupart de l'Espagne ou du Mexique, ont considérablement changé la vie des autochtones. Sans les Espagnols, ne seraient jamais nés l'art des bijoux en argent et la fabrication de couvertures colorées qu'ont développés les Navajo et les Hopis.

Environ un dizième de l'Arizona appartient encore ou plutôt de nouveau au peuple Indien. Le gouvernement américain a remis entre les mains des NAVAJOS et des HOPIS presque toute l'administration de leurs réserves. Ces tribus étaient bien plus évoluées que les aborigènes primitifs de Californie. Quelque deux mille membres réchappèrent à la guerre meurtrière engagée contre les Indiens. En l'escape de cent ans, leur nombre est passé à deux cent mille. Les Navajos ont depuis regagné les territoires dont ils avaient été chassés et leur taux de natalité augmente d'année en année. Par contre, la population des Hopis n'a fait que doubler durant la même période. Environ trois mille vivent aujourd'hui dans une réserve relativement modeste au sein de celle des Navajos. Pourtant, ces deux peuples sont très éloignés l'un de l'autre par leurs coutumes et leur langage.

Une grande partie des merveilles naturelles du Sud-Ouest américain est située dans la Monument Valley. Témoins en sont les photographies de cet ouvrage. A l'origine, la région était un plateau rocheux de quelque mille cinq cents mètres de hauteur. Au cours de millions d'années, la glace, l'eau et les fontes de neige érodèrent le sol mais ne firent que ronger les couches de roche. Il en a résulté un paysage étrange de tours et d'aiguilles déchiquetées se dressant entre des bouches de grottes monumentales. Une stupeur admirative saisit à chaque pas, alors qu'en fin de compte, le regard n'a enregistré qu'une infime partie du spectacle grandiose de la nature.

Quelques centaines de familles vivent durant l'été dans le canyon de Chelly, situé sur la réserve des Navajos. Elles habitent presque toutes dans des «hogans» répliques exactes de ceux que leurs ancêtres occupaient il y a des siècles de cela. Ces demeures sont des huttes hexagonales ou octogonales, construites en troncs massifs et recouvertes de terre ou de couches d'herbe. Le canyon Chelly, gorge interminable aux parois abruptes, abrite des cavernes, des habitations troglodytiques où les Indiens venaient se réfugier durant les périodes de danger. Leurs murs, recouverts de mystérieux symboles peints sont très bien conservés.

D'autres abris, longs parfois de plusieurs centaines de mètres, ont été creusés dans les parois verticales des cavernes. On les trouve à l'intérieur des ravins des Mesas qui se dressent jusqu'à deux mille cinq cents mètres. Les Mesas ou tables en

espagnol, sont des plateaux séparés par de profondes vallées escarpées. Les anciens troglodytes vivaient de la culture des champs et de la cueillette de plantes sauvages qui poussaient dans les ravins. En cas de danger, ils grimpaient à des échelles pour se réfugier dans les cavernes, faciles à défendre. Ils y avaient amassé des réserves de provisions et l'eau de source coulait en abondance. On a compté jusqu'à deux cent cinquante pièces différentes dans quelques-unes des habitations troglodytiques. Grâce à des analyses du carbone quatorze, il a été possible de déterminer que la civilisation des mesas a connu son apogée du onzième au milieu du quatorzième siècle. A cette époque déjà, les légendaires «Anasazi», les Anciens, étaient à l'œuvre. On ignore toutefois pourquoi à la même période, les Indiens quittèrent les habitations des grottes.

L'Utah possède également une foule de merveilles de la nature que l'Etat a prises sous sa protection. On y trouve un nombre stupéfiant de PONTS NATURELS. Le site protégé «ARCHES NATIONALPARK» en compte quatre-vingt-neuf à lui seul. Les cours d'eau ont disparu au fil des siècles et ces ponts franchissent aujourd'hui des précipices dont la largeur et la profondeur atteignent cinquante mètres. Les ponts sont si étroits et minces qu'on ose à peine s'y engager.

Les forces de la nature ont créé des spectacles somptueux au cours de millions d'années et elles sont toujours à l'œuvre. On peut classer le BRYCE CANYON au sud-est de l'Utah parmi les merveilles naturelles incomparables. Ses tours de rochers meurtris, ensanglantées au lever et au coucher du soleil, se dressent dans un paysage sauvage et désertique. Malgré la quasi-inaccessibilité de la région, les pères espagnols avaient découvert le Bryce canyon en 1776 et mis en garde contre sa nature sauvage. Les trappeurs américains arrivèrent en 1821 et les MORMONS de l'Utah y fondèrent leurs colonies en 1864.

Le site le plus gigantesque du Sud-Ouest est sans aucun doute le GRAND CANYON, une gorge du Colorado dont les parois atteignent mille six cents mètres de profondeur. LOPEZ DE CARDENAS, membre de l'expédition de Francisco Coronado, découvrait déjà en 1542 cette merveille du monde. Même les photographies les pius sophistiquées ne peuvent reproduire les jeux fulgurants des effets de lumière au lever et au coucher du soleil.

La VALLÉE HAVASU, bien que moins connue, est presque plus intéressante à mon humble avis. Les INDIENS HAVASUPAI, dont on pourrait traduire le nom par «les hommes de l'eau verte», vivent dans cet étroit ravin à la végétation luxuriante. C'est dans cette région magnifique que s'étendent leurs réserves et ils acceptent quelquefois de recevoir un nombre restreint de visiteurs. On accède aux villages à dos de mulets si l'ascension est permise. Mais il faut veiller à ne laisser aucun détritus sur le trajet!

Mon séjour s'achève à l'aéroport de BORREGO SPRINGS où je dois prendre un avion pour Los Angeles et ensuite regagner mon cher Munich via Frankfurt. Un Cessna de quatre-vingts places suffit pour le saut qu'il y a à faire de BORREGO à LA. L'appareil, annoncé toutes les cinq minutes, n'arrive pourtant pas. L'unique employé du mini-aéroport avoue alors, qu'une fois de plus, le brouillard empêche l'atterissage du Cessna. Un autre voyageur attend également avec impatience.

«Ça arrive toujours dans ce pays» gronde l'homme d'un certain âge, à la haute stature et aux traits marquants. Son expression traduit l'ennui, mais son regard brille d'énergie.

«Il est plus facile de voler vers la lune que d'ici à LA» grogne encore mon compagnon d'infortune. «On part à l'heure précise et on arrive à la minute!»

Je souriais déjà de la plaisanterie absurde quand l'employé derrière le guichet m'avertit d'un regard.

«Plaisanterie mise à part, Monsieur a raison», dit-il. «Vous parlez à Neil Armstrong, le premier homme à avoir posé le pied sur la lune. C'était le 21 juillet 1969 ...»

El Camino Real

San Diego de Alcala was the first Franciscan mission to be founded in the area that we now call California. A half-starved expedition arrived there in 1796 after a two-month journey from Loreto in Spanish Mexico. More than half of the group of 219 lost their lives on the long journey; of the survivors, three monks, eight soldiers and two dozen pioneers founded the mission and settlement of San Diego de Alcala. Within twenty years, nearly 30,000 acres of land had come under cultivation: there were 1250 horses, 10,000 cattle, 20,000 sheep and even vineyards. Today it is simply known as San Diego, city of over a million inhabitants. San Diego was the first of a chain of Spanish missions stretching for six hundred miles across the state. They were constructed between 1769 and 1822, when the last, San Francisco de Solano, was founded. The so-called El Camino Real, the king's highway, connected all 21 mission posts. Los Angeles, today the third largest city in the USA, possessed a modest 47 inhabitants at its birth; to make up for this, it boasted the extraordinarily lengthy name of El Pueblo de la Nuestra Señora la Reina de Los Angeles de Porciuncala.

San Diego de Alcala war die erste Mission des Franziskaner-Ordens im heutigen Kalifornien. Dort erschien 1769 eine halbverhungerte Expedition, die zwei Monate zuvor in Loreto, Spanisch Mexico, aufgebrochen war. Mehr als die Hälfte der 219 Teilnehmer war auf dem weiten Weg ums Leben gekommen. Drei der überlebenden Mönche, acht Soldaten und zwei Dutzend Siedler gründeten sogleich die Mission und Siedlung San Diego de Alcala. Nach zwanzig Jahren gab es dort 12 000 Hektar bebautes Land, 1250 Pferde, 10 000 Rinder, 20 000 Schafe und auch Weinberge. Die heutige Millionenstadt San Diego ist daraus entstanden. 1769 war San Diego der Anfang und 1822 San Francisco de Solano das Ende der ungefähr 1000 Kilometer langen Kette spanischer Missionen im heutigen US-Staat Kalifornien. Aus insgesamt 21 Stationen bestand der sogenannte Camino Real, der Königsweg. Als Los Angeles, heute drittgrößte Stadt der Vereinigten Staaten, gegründet wurde, gab es dort nur 47 Bewohner. Dafür war der ursprüngliche Name ellenlang: El Pueblo de la Nuestra Señora la Reina de Los Angeles de Porciuncala!

San Diego de Alcala a été la première Mission fondée par l'Ordre des Franciscains dans l'actuelle Californie. C'est là qu'est apparue, en 1769, une expédition à moitié morte de faim, partie deux mois plus tôt de Loreto, en espagnol Mexico. Plus de la moitié des 219 membres de l'expédition avaient péri en cours de route. Trois des moines survivants, huit soldats et une bonne vingtaine de colons ont fondé la Mission et point de peuplement de San Diego de Alcala. Vingt ans plus tard, San Diego comptait 12 000 hectares de terres cultivées, 1250 chevaux, 10 000 bovins, 20 000 moutons. C'est à partir de ce noyau que s'est développée par la suite l'actuelle ville de San Diego, une agglomération de plus d'un million d'habitants. C'est de San Diego, fondé en 1769, que s'est développée jusqu'à San Francisco de Solano, fondé en 1822, la longue chaîne des Missions espagnoles de l'actuel Etat américain de Californie. Long en effet de 1000 kilomètres, le Camino Real, la voie Royale, comprenait au total 21 stations. Au moment de sa fondation, Los Angeles, troisième ville des Etats-Unis à l'heure actuelle, ne comptait que 47 habitants. Son nom, par contre, n'en finissait pas: El Pueblo de la Nuestra Senora la Reina de Los Angeles de Porciuncala!

page 33: San Diego de Alcala

Mission Santa Barbara "Queen of the Missions"

Mission San Juan Capistrano

Spanish Caretta – 19th c. transportation for the mission

Mission San Luis Rey de Francia

Mission Santa Cruz

Mission San Rafael Arcángel

Mission Gabriel Arcángel, Los Angeles

Mission San Carlos Borromeo de Carmelo, Carmel

Mission San Francisco de Asis (Dolores)

Mission San Francisco de Solano

El Camino Real

FROM SAN DIEGO TO SAN FRANCISCO

Some missions have survived to this day, others have been carefully restored as authentically as possible. They all bear a superficial resemblance to each other, although they all have their own often turbulent history. Some have excellent museums within their precincts. Most of the Spanish Catholic churches are once again in use; many of their old bells were cast in Russian foundries in Alaska. The mission of St Gabriel was the nucleus of the modern city of Los Angeles and Dolores de San Francisco eventually became the large and flourishing trading centre of San Francisco.

Die noch erhaltenen, auch die originalgetreu wiederhergestellten Missionen sind, äußerlich betrachtet, einander ähnlich. Dennoch hat jede ihre eigene, oft sehr bewegte Geschichte. Manche besitzen hinter ihren Mauern sehenswerte Museen der alten Zeit. Die meisten der spanisch-katholischen Kirchen sind heute wieder in Gebrauch, viele der alten Glocken wurden von russischen Werkmeistern in Alaska gegossen. Die Mission San Gabriel war Keimzelle der heutigen Millionenstadt Los Angeles, und aus Dolores de San Francisco wurde die große, blühende Handelsstadt San Francisco.

Les Missions, celles qui ont été préservées tout comme celles qui ont été reconstruites ou restaurées dans le style d'origine, se ressemblent extérieurement. Elles ont cependant toutes leur propre histoire, une histoire bien souvent mouvementée. Certaines d'entre elles abritent derrière leurs murs des musées de l'ancien temps qui méritent que l'on s'y attarde. La majorité des églises catholiques d'origine espagnole servent de nouveau aujourd'hui à la célébration du culte; un grand nombre des vieilles cloches sont l'œuvre d'artisans russes d'Alaska. La Mission San Gabriel a donné naissance à l'actuelle ville de Los Angeles, comptant près de trois millions d'habitants; Dolores de San Francisco est devenu la grande ville commerciale florissante de San Francisco.

CALIFORNIA
Los Angeles
OLVERA STREET and the CITY HALL

OLVERA STREET, in the centre of Los Angeles, the city of millions. This was the heart of a lively little community of seventy-four inhabitants that was founded as "El Pueblo de Nostra Senora la Reina de Los Angeles de Porciuncula". Fifty-four letters is a long name for a small settlement; it is still the official name of a city which is now sixty-two miles wide, and which nowadays the Angelos simply call L.A. Los Angeles' imposing CITY HALL is situated on a now overcrowded hill near Olvera Street. It is not a hundred years ago that, in accordance with a brutal lynch law, horse thieves were hanged from the branches of a group of trees on the hill.

Die OLVERA-STRASSE im Zentrum der Vielmillionenstadt Los Angeles war in der ersten Zeit nach Gründung von „El Pueblo de Nuestra Senora la Reine de Los Angeles de Porciuncula" das lebhaft pulsierende Herz der kleinen Siedlung von zunächst nur siebenundvierzig Bewohnern. Dafür enthielt der offiziell bis heute geltende Name fünfundfünfzig Buchstaben. Aber die Angelos nennen ihre fast hundert Kilometer breite Stadt kurz und schlicht L.A. Die CITY HALL, das imposante Rathaus von L.A., erhebt sich auf dem nun überbauten Hügel nahe der Olvera Street. Es sind noch keine hundert Jahre vergangen, seitdem man an den Ästen einer dort oben vorhandenen Baumgruppe, im Rahmen einer strengen Lynchjustiz, die Pferdediebe aufgehängt hat.

Après la fondation de «El Pueblo de Nuestra Senora la Reine de Los Angeles de Porciuncula» LA RUE OLVERA était au début, le centre grouillant de vie de la petite commune qui ne comptait alors que 47 habitants. Les Angelos surnomment tout simplement L.A. leur ville qu s'étend sur près de cent kilomètres. LE CITY HALL, l'imposant Hôtel de ville de L.A., se dresse près de la rue Olvera, sur une colline noyée aujourd'hui sous les constructions. Il y a à peine un siècle, une sévère justice de lynchage faisait pendre les voleurs de chevaux aux arbres qui poussaient sur cette colline.

36

Los Angeles

It is when the city lights go on that one begins to grasp the unbelievably vast extent of Los Angeles. It would take a good four days of fast marching to cross the city on foot, along streets whose house numbers sometimes exceed 2000. Nevertheless, not everything that is shown in this night photo comes under the administration of City Hall, for the original Spanish settlement of Los Angeles comprised dozens of small colonies, some of which joined up to form independent boroughs. The unwary traveller who assumes that he can telephone for the price of a local call within this sea of buildings will often find that he has made, and what's more has to pay for, a long-distance call.

Wenn alle Lichter brennen, erkennt man so recht die unglaublich weite Ausdehnung von Los Angeles. Wer die Stadt in ganzer Breite durchwandern wollte, müßte dazu vier Tage lang flott marschieren. Bei manchen Straßen reichen die Hausnummern bis über zweitausend. Aber nicht alles, was diese Nachtaufnahme zeigt, wird von der Stadtverwaltung in der City Hall regiert. Weil das historische, das ursprünglich spanische Los Angeles aus vielen Dutzend kleinen Siedlungen entstanden ist, sind heute noch viele der längst zusammengewachsenen Stadtviertel eigene Gemeinden geblieben. Wer in L.A. telefoniert, muß wissen, daß er auch innerhalb des Häusermeeres oft Ferngespräche führt und bezahlen muß.

On réalise l'incroyable étendue de L.A., le soir, quand les lumières s'allument. Il faudrait quatre jours à un bon marcheur pour parcourir la ville dans toute sa largeur. Les numéros des maisons dépassent deux mille dans quelques rues. Mais tout ce que cette prise de vue nocturne montre, n'est pas entièrement administré par la municipalité. Le Los Angeles historique, espagnol à l'origine, est né de douzaines de petites agglomérations. Bien des quartiers de la ville qui se fondent aujourd'hui sont donc restés des communes indépendantes.

Coastline/Big Sur

Steep cliffs and a sandy bathing beach together in one bay; there is no limit to the variety of landscapes to be found along the Pacific coast. In an east wind, gigantic breakers will thunder against steep cliffs, where only a few days later there are mere wavelets rippling over the pale sand. In the background all sorts of colourful, exotic and thorny plants blossom and flourish on the slopes of the coastal mountains.

Steile Küsten und sandiger Badestrand, beides in der gleichen Bucht. Jede nur mögliche Landschaft hat Kalifornien am Rand des Pazifischen Ozeans zu bieten. Wenn starker Ostwind weht, donnert die Brandung mit gewaltigen Brechern gegen die Felsmauern, aber wenige Tage später sind es nur noch sanfte Wellen auf hellem Sand. Dahinter, am Hang der Küstenberge, gedeiht und blüht eine Vielfalt bunter, exotischer und stacheliger Pflanzen.

Côtes abruptes et plage de sable fin dans la même baie. La Californie offre toutes les sortes possibles de paysages en bordure de l'Océan Pacifique. Quand le vent d'Est est assez fort, les flots viennent se fendre avec violence contre les parois rocheuses; mais quelques jours plus tard, il n'y a plus que quelques vagues légères qui clapotent sur le sable clair. Plus loin, sur les coteaux du littoral fleurit une multitude de plantes de toutes les couleurs, épineuses et exotiques.

page 41: Flowering Yucca (which can reach a height of over 13 feet) in the San Gabriel Mountains near Los Angeles.

Coastline/Big Sur
BRIDGE OVER BIXBY CREEK

The bridge over Bixby Creek is famous for its daring construction, for it spans an extremely deep, almost vertically-sided gorge with a turbulent stream below. In front are the rugged cliffs of the coast, battered by the almost constant surging of the Pacific. The coast road above is reckoned to have a landscape second to none in the world, and the author can only nod in agreement. It is the State highway no. 1, commonly known as the Big Sur. Only a few scattered settlements lie along its course, for farms, fields and fruits have little chance of survival on the barren thorny scrub of the High Chapparal behind. This explains the small population in such a beautiful area.

Weithin berühmt ist die Brücke über den Bixby Creek wegen ihrer kühnen Konstruktion, denn sie überspannt eine sehr tiefe, fast senkrechte Schlucht mit tosendem Wildbach. Davor die zerklüftete Steilküste mit der fast immer schäumenden Brandung des Pazifischen Ozeans. Die Straße darüber gilt, meines Erachtens mit Recht, als eine der landschaftlich schönsten der Welt. Es ist die US-Bundesstraße Nr. 1 an der Big Sur. Weil die Berge und Hügel dahinter nur kargen Boden bieten, zum großen Teil mit Dorngestrüpp, dem sogenannten Chapparal, bewachsen, konnten sich Farmen, Weidebetrieb und Obstplantagen nicht entwickeln. Also ist die schöne Gegend nur wenig besiedelt und auf weiten Strecken auch menschenleer.

Le Pont qui franchit la Bixby Creek est célèbre de par sa construction audacieuse. Il surpombe un ravin très profond, aux parois presque à pic, au fond duquel gronde un torrent. Devant, les falaises déchiquetées où vient s'écraser le déferlement écumeux de l'Océan Pacifique. La route au-dessus passe pour une des plus belles du monde et c'est bien mon avis également. C'est la Nationale I, connue sous le nom de Big Sur. Comme l'élevage, les plantations fruitières, l'agriculture ne peuvent prospérer, sur son sol inculte, cette belle région est dépeuplée et offre souvent des étendues où l'on ne voit âme qui vive.

45

Coastline near Monterey

The Bay of Monterey is one of the most beautiful places on earth. The visitor can take home a lifetime's memory of the stupendous views to be found north and south along the coast. The state highway no. 1, completed in 1937 at the Big Sur, is a challenge to the motorist with its constant twists and turns, but parking places every few miles provide an opportunity to stretch one's legs and enjoy the dramatic scenery and the glorious sight of the flowering wild plants at one's leisure.

Die Küste bei Monterey gehört zu den schönsten Stellen unserer Welt. Viele Meilen weit im Norden wie Süden bietet die Küste so viele wunderbare Ausblicke, daß sich der Besucher zeitlebens daran erinnert. Die 1937 vollendete Staatsstraße Nr. 1 an der Big Sur ist wegen ihrer zahlreichen Spitzkehren nicht leicht zu befahren. Aber es gibt alle paar Meilen Standplätze fürs Verweilen. Von dort aus bewundert man in aller Ruhe die fabelhafte Landschaft und die Pracht der blühenden Wildpflanzen.

La baie de Monterey compte parmi les plus belles de la terre. Sur des kilomètres et des kilomètres, que ce soit vers le Nord ou le Sud, la côte offre une telle quantité de panoramas merveilleux qu'ils resteront gravés à tout jamais dans la mémoire des visiteurs. Achevée en 1937, la route nationale 1, qui longe le Big Sur, est une route difficile en raison de ses nombreux virages en épingle à cheveux. Mais tous les quinze ou vingt kilomètres, il est possible de faire une pause sur des terre-pleins prévus à cet effet et d'admirer en toute tranquillité le fabuleux paysage et la splendeur des plantes sauvages en fleur.

page 47: The ECHEVERIA plant grows around the coasts at sea level.

CALIFORNIA
Coastline near Monterey

The coast that extends around Monterey is unique. The shore is never peaceful, but always battered by the onslaught of waves. In spite of the storms, weatherbeaten spruce and shrubs have gained a foothold on the cliffs and there is a carpet of flourishing vegetation and flowering plants, among them alpine stonecrop.

Wie keine andere ist die Küste in der weiteren Umgebung von Monterey! In den Uferfelsen halten sich trotz aller Stürme zerzauste Fichten und anderes Gehölz. Nie herrscht Ruhe am Meeresrand, immer rauscht die Brandung. Überall wildwachsende Vegetation und bunte Blumen, darunter auch blühendes Sedum.

Il n'existe nulle part ailleurs de côte semblable à celle des environs de Monterey. Dans les rochers longeant le rivage, des épicéas «ébouriffés» et autres arbres bravent les tempêtes. Il ne fait jamais calme au bord de la mer, il y a toujours le bruit des vagues qui viennent déferler. Partout une végétation sauvage, des fleurs de toutes les couleurs, avec également de l'orpin fleuri.

page 49: BALD EAGLE/Weißkopfseeadler/Pygargue à tête blanche (Haliaeetus leucocephalus)

CALIFORNIA
Point Lobos

At the foot of the precipitous cliffs below the Big Sur, especially towards the northern end of this magnificent Pacific coastal route, an increasing number of protected sea mammals are able to lead an undisturbed life. There are many species; one can see fur seals, sea lions, seals and in certain areas the massive bulks of sea-elephants. With luck and a good pair of binoculars it is even possible to spot little schools of sea otters amid the drifting clumps of seaweed. Other animals are also gradually becoming less rare here; walruses, sperm whales, grey whales and even the giant blue whales.

Am Fuße der Steilküste unterhalb der Big Sur, besonders nahe dem nördlichen Ende dieser herrlich schönen pazifischen Küstenstraße, leben ungestört und gesetzlich geschützt eine ständig zunehmende Zahl von Säugetieren des Meeres. Ganz verschiedene Arten sind vertreten, unter anderem Pelzrobben, Seelöwen, Seehunde und auch an verschiedenen Stellen die tonnenschweren See-Elefanten. Wer Glück hat und ein gutes Fernglas, wird inmitten treibenden Seetangs auch ein kleines Volk der Seeotter entdecken. Es gibt Walrosse an der Pazifischen Küste, Pottwale, Grauwale, und sogar die Blauwale, die größten Tiere auf Erden, nehmen langsam wieder an Zahl zu.

Au pied des falaises, au-dessous du Big Sur et surtout au bout de la partie nord de cette merveilleuse route qui longe le littoral pacifique, vivent en paix et protégés par des lois, des mammifères marins au nombre toujours croissant. On y trouve de multiples espèces dont des phoques, des otaries, des veaux marins et à différents endroits, des éléphants de mer lourds de plusieurs tonnes. Des chevaux marins, des baleines grises habitent aussi les côtes du Pacifique et le nombre des baleines bleues, les plus grands animaux terriens, s'accroît également tout doucement.

page 51:   SEA LIONS/Californische Seelöwen/Lions de mer (Zalaphus californianus)
page 52/53: Peninsula Monterey

CALIFORNIA
San Francisco

For half a century, the GOLDEN GATE BRIDGE has been the great attraction of San Francisco. It was constructed between 1933 and 1937, of sufficient length (4,600 ft.) and height (246 ft.) to allow even the largest merchant navy vessels and warships into San Francisco harbour, and it cost 35 million of the good old, long-vanished, gold dollars. The steel towers on each side are 820 ft. high and are reputed to be the highest of their kind in the world.

Schon seit einem halben Jahrhundert ist die größte Sehenswürdigkeit von San Francisco die GOLDEN GATE BRIDGE, die Brücke übers Goldene Tor. Sie mußte so hoch (75 Meter) und so weitgespannt (1400 Meter) sein, damit auch die größten Schiffe der Handelsmarine und Kriegsflotte darunter die San-Francisco-Bucht passieren können. Gebaut wurde das Wunderwerk von 1933 bis 1937 zum Preise von 35 Millionen damals noch guter, goldener Dollars. Die Stahltürme auf beiden Seiten sollen mit 250 Metern die höchsten Brückenpfeiler der Welt sein.

Depuis un demi-siècle déjà, LE PONT DU GOLDEN GATE (Golden Gate Bridge) constitue la plus grande curiosité de San Francisco. Il fallait qu'il ait une hauteur (75 mètres) et une largeur (1400 mètres) suffisantes pour que les plus grands bâtiments de la marine marchande et les navires de guerre puissent franchir la baie de San Francisco. Construite de 1933 à 1937, cette petite merveille a coûté 35 millions de dollars de l'époque, des dollars encore sonnants et trébuchants. Avec leurs 250 mètres, les piliers soutenant le pont sont, paraît-il, les plus hauts du monde.

page 54: San Francisco, Golden Gate Bridge.
page 55: San Francisco, Steiner Street and
downtown skyline.

CALIFORNIA
San Francisco

The Franciscan Mission which was founded in 1776 beside the lagoon of Nuestra Señora de los Dolores was originally given the name of San Francisco de Asis. Later known simply as the MISSION DOLORES, it is now part of the enormous, beautiful and wealthy city of San Francisco. The first church and some parts of the mission, including the old Spanish cemetery, still stand. Next to them a baroque cathedral was built to cater for the rapidly increasing population. There was a brilliantly organised World Fair here in 1915, and parts of the PALACE OF FINE ARTS, looking more like Roman remains than anything else, are still to be seen.

San Francisco de Asis hieß bei ihrer Gründung 1776 die Mission der Franziskaner an der Lagune de Nuestra Señora de los Dolores. Aber mit der Zeit wurde daraus der kurze Name MISSION DOLORES. Eine riesige, sehr schöne und reiche Stadt entstand daraus, nämlich San Francisco. Die erste Kirche und Teile der Mission, sogar der altspanische Friedhof sind noch vorhanden. Daneben aber wurde wegen der rasch zunehmenden Zahl der Bewohner eine barocke Kathedrale gebaut. Von der glänzend organisierten Weltausstellung im Jahre 1915 sind noch die altrömisch wirkenden Bauten des PALASTES DER SCHÖNEN KÜNSTE geblieben.

San Francisco de Asis était le nom de la Mission fondée par les Franciscains dans la lagune de Nuestra Senora de los Dolores en 1776. Mais avec le temps, le nom s'est racourci: MISSION DOLORES. Elle a donné naissance à une ville belle, immense et riche, San Francisco. Il reste encore aujourd'hui la première église, certaines parties de la Mission et même le cimetière espagnol. Mais pour faire face à une population toujours croissante, l'on a construit juste à côté une Eglise baroque. De l'Exposition Mondiale de 1915, il reste encore les bâtiments à caractère romain du PALAIS DES BEAUX-ARTS.

page 56: The mission of San Francisco de Asis (Dolores)
page 57: San Francisco, Palace of Fine Arts.

CALIFORNIA
San Francisco

San Francisco is a garden city which has as its centre the enormous and superbly-kept Golden Gate Park. The layout of the town was determined by its position on a rocky peninsula and sometimes necessitated quite bizarre road building methods, for instance in Lombard Street. The old fishing harbour is well worth a visit, not only on account of its ocean-going vessels but also for its many fish restaurants.

Eine Gartenstadt ist San Francisco, mit dem überaus großen, aufs beste gepflegten Golden-Gate-Park in der Mitte. Die Lage der Stadt, zum größten Teil auf steilaufragender Halbinsel, hat den Bau recht abenteuerlicher Straßen notwendig gemacht, wie beispielsweise die Lombard Street. Keinesfalls übersehen sollte man den alten Fischereihafen, wo nicht nur die hochseetüchtigen Boote liegen, sondern viele Fischrestaurants.

Avec son immense Golden Gate Park, extrêmement soigné, en plein centre, San Francisco est une ville de jardins et de parcs. Comme la ville est située en majeure partie sur une péninsule à pentes abruptes, il a fallu construire des rues bien souvent tortueuses comme par exemple la Lombard Street. Il faut aller voir le vieux port de pêche qui n'abrite pas que les bâteaux de haute mer mais également une quantité de restaurants spécialisés dans les plats de poissons.

page 58:   San Francisco, Lombard Street.
page 59:   San Francisco; cable car on Hyde Street, showing Fisherman's Wharf and the prison island of Alcatraz.
Pages 60/61: San Francisco from the Twin Peaks: view downtown showing Market Street, San Francisco Bay and Oakland Bridge.

Napa Valley

WINE COUNTRY

We must give credit to the pious friars for many of the things that make life enjoyable in present-day California. Spanish vines, generally assumed to have originated in Ancient Greece, were imported to the Californian missions via Mexico and the South American colonies of the Spanish empire. It was not until the second half of the last century that the wine-growing potential of the slopes north of San Francisco was fully recognised. French, Italian and German vintners have made a great contribution to the successful development of the Californian wine industry.

Wie bei so vielen Wohltaten, die man heute in Kalifornien genießen kann, haben auch beim Wein die frommen Mönche den Anfang gemacht. Sie brachten spanische Weinstöcke, deren Ursprung man im antiken Griechenland vermutet, über Mexiko und die südamerikanischen Kolonien des spanischen Weltreichs bis nach Kalifornien. Aber erst in der zweiten Hälfte des vorigen Jahrhunderts stellte sich heraus, daß vor allem die Berghänge nördlich von San Francisco für den Anbau besonders günstig waren. Der Kalifornische Wein hat sich dank der Bemühungen französischer, italienischer und deutscher Winzer großartig entwickelt.

Comme pour un grand nombre de bonnes choses que la Californie vous offre, ce sont les moines qui, en matière de vin également, ont fait œuvre de pionnier. Par le Mexique et les colonies sud-américaines de l'Empire espagnol, ils ont amené jusqu'en Californie des sortes de ceps de vigne qui devaient déjà exister dans l'Antiquité grecque. Mais ce n'est que dans la seconde moitié du 19ème siècle que certains coteaux, en particulier ceux au Nord de San Francisco, se sont avérés spécialement favorables à la viticulture. Grâce aux efforts de viticulteurs français, italiens et allemands.

CALIFORNIA
Yosemite
NATIONAL PARK

The Yosemite National Park is yet another of California's unrivalled achievements. It was the world's first protected area for wildlife. President Lincoln passed the original law in 1864, when the Civil War was still raging. Although the law was not enforced until 1870 and the planned extensions and development lasted until 1903, it is nevertheless due to President Lincoln that Yosemite, encompassing an area of nearly 1,240 square miles, is now the most beautiful National Park in California.

Zu den vielen Superlativen in Kalifornien gehört bestimmt der Yosemite-National-Park. Er war das erste Naturschutzgebiet der Welt. Schon 1864, mitten im amerikanischen Bürgerkrieg, hat Präsident Lincoln das Gesetz zu seinem Schutz unterschrieben. Zwar hat die Durchführung noch bis 1870, haben die Erweiterungen und hat die Erschließung noch bis 1903 gedauert, aber ohne Abraham Lincoln wäre Yosemite nicht der schönste kalifornische Nationalpark mit 3205 Quadratkilometern Ausdehnung geworden.

Parmi les nombreux superlatifs de la Californie figure sans aucun doute le Parc National de Yosemite. Il a été le premier parc du monde à avoir été classé comme site naturel protégé. Dès 1864, en pleine guerre civile américaine, le Président Abraham Lincoln a signé loi en ce sens. Il faudra, certes, attendre 1870 pour qu'elle entre en vigueur et 1903 pour que le parc soit agrandi et aménagé. Il n'empêche que sans Abraham Lincoln, jamais le Parc Yosemite, avec ses 3205 kilomètres carrés, ne serait devenu le plus beau parc naturel de Californie.

page 64: Glacier Point looking over to the Yosemite Falls

Yosemite National Park
MERCED RIVER

Shortly after the end of the last ice age, people arrived to inhabit the green valleys on the banks of the foaming rivers. In 1838 the first trappers and fur dealers appeared from the USA – illegally, needless to say, for first the Spanish and then the Mexican governments had banned all outsiders from entering California. Their presence there was seen as a threat by the natives, jeopardising as it did the existence of the animals which had always been their means of subsistence. The National Parks of California can boast dozens of magnificent waterfalls to delight their visitors. This one falls in three stages, starting in bleak mountain scenery and descending into a dense forest.

Menschen haben schon bald nach der letzten Eiszeit in den grünen Tälern am Rande der schäumenden Flüsse gewohnt. Weiße Trapper und Pelzhändler aus den USA erschienen erst 1838, illegal natürlich. Die Eingeborenen fühlten sich bedroht, denn die Fremden waren eine Gefahr für die Tierwelt, von der seit undenklichen Zeiten die Indianer lebten. Viele Dutzend herrlicher Wasserfälle bieten die Naturschutzgebiete Kaliforniens ihren Besuchern. In drei Stufen stürzt dieser Fall vom kahlen Hochgebirge in den tiefgrünen Wald.

Juste après la troisième glaciation, des hommes ont habité les vertes vallées longeant les fleuves tempêtueux. Ce n'est qu'à partir de 1838 que des trappeurs et des fourreurs blancs sont arrivés des Etats-Unis. Les indigènes se sont sentis menacés; les étrangers, en effet, constituaient un danger pour le monde animal dans lequel les Indiens vivaient depuis des temps immémorables. Les parcs protégés de Californie offrent aux visiteurs des douzaines de merveilleuses chutes d'eau. Sur trois paliers, elles se précipitent des hautes montagnes arides dans la verdure des forêts.

pages 66/67: "El Capitan" and "Merced River"
page 68: Yosemite National Park, California
page 69: The Bridal Veil Waterfall

CALIFORNIA
Yosemite
NATIONAL PARK

It was the usual pattern; the natives were driven out and exterminated. These days the animals and the landscape are strictly protected by law. The park is open to visitors throughout the year, although the roads are often blocked by snow between October and May. It is unfortunately impossible to describe all the attractions of Yosemite, and the tourist is recommended to visit one of the Visitors' Centers at each of the four entrances to the park for a comprehensive information service.

Es geschah das gleiche wie schon oft, nämlich die Vertreibung und Ausrottung der Eingeborenen. Nun aber sind alle Tiere im Park und auch die gesamte Landschaft streng geschützt. Zwar ist der Park während des ganzen Jahres fürs Publikum geöffnet, aber von Oktober bis Mai werden sehr oft die Straßen von Schnee blockiert. Leider fehlt es an Platz, um alle Schönheiten des Yosemite aufzuzählen. Es ist für den Besucher viel einfacher, sich in einem der „Visitors Centers" an den vier Eingängen des Schutzgebietes schriftliche und mündliche Informationen zu beschaffen.

Les indigènes connuvent le même sort que partout ailleurs: ils furent chassés et exterminés. Aujourd'hui, des lois assez strictes sur la protection de l'environnement permettent de préserver nature et animaux. Le Parc est ouvert toute l'année au public, certes; mais d'octobre à mai, les routes sont très souvent bloquées par la neige. La place manque, malheureusement, pour énumérer toutes les beautés du Parc National de Yosémite. Il est beaucoup plus simple pour le visiteur de se procurer les informations voulues aux «Visitors Centers» situés à chacune des quatre entrées du Parc.

National Parks
ANIMALS OF THE WILDERNESS

The elk is the largest and most powerful of the red deer. It migrates to the hills in summer and returns tho the valleys in winter, preferring fairly open terrain. Its enormous 12 – pointed antlers can weigh up to forty-four pounds.

Der Elk (Wapitihirsch) ist der größte und stärkste unter den Rothirschen, zieht im Sommer in die Berge und kommt zur Winterzeit wieder in die Täler zurück. Er bevorzugt halboffenes Gelände. Das mächtige Geweih, das in der Regel nur 12 Enden hat, kann ein Gewicht von über 20 kg erreichen.

Le cerf Wapiti est le plus grand et le plus fort des animaux de la famille des cervidés. Il migre dans les montagnes durant l'été et revient dans les vallées à l'approche de l'hiver. Il préfère des terrains mi-ouverts. Ses bois impressionnants qui ne portent normalement que douze ramifications, peuvent atteindre un poids au-dessus de 20 kilogrammes.

page 71: ELK/Wapitihirsch/Wapiti (Cervus canadensis)

Kings Canyon/Sequoia
NATIONAL PARK

Not only in Yosemite is it possible to make a pilgrimage to the world's most massive living things, but also in the Sequoia and King's Canyon National Parks. These two parks are adjacent and together cover an area nearly as great as that of Yosemite; in the middle is Mount Whitney, the highest mountain in the 48 contiguous states. The most important feature is, however, Redwood Park, where the incomparable sequoia (Sequoiadendron giganteum) and the taller, slimmer coast redwood (Sequoia sempervirens) grow.

Die schwersten und dicksten Lebewesen der Welt bestaunt der Besucher Kaliforniens nicht nur im Yosemite-Park, sondern auch im Sequoia- und im Kings-Canyon-Nationalpark. Beide Schutzgebiete haben fast die gleiche Ausdehnung wie der Yosemite und erreichen mit dem Mount Whitney den höchsten Punkt der Vereinigten Staaten, nur Alaska ausgenommen. Wichtiger noch, mit nichts anderem zu vergleichen, die schwere Sequoia gigantea und ihre schlanke, noch höher steigende Schwester Sequoia sempervirens, die sich weit droben im Redwood Park befindet.

Ce n'est pas seulement dans le Parc de Yosemite mais également dans les deux autres parcs nationaux de Sequoia et de Kings Canyon qu'il est possible d'admirer les êtres vivants les plus lourds du monde. Ces deux parcs ont à peu près la même superficie que le parc de Yosemite et représentent avec le Mont Whitney le point culminant des Etats-Unis et du continent nord-américain (Alaska non compris). Mais il y a plus caractéristique encore: deux sortes d'arbre, uniques en leur genre, le lourd Sequoia gigantum et un conifére voisin, plus mince et plus grand encore, le «Sequoia sempervirens» qui se trouvent plus haut, dans le Parc National de Redwood.

CALIFORNIA
Kings Canyon/Sequoia
NATIONAL PARK

The Libby tree reaches a height of over 300 ft. Standing next to the "General Sherman" in the Giant Forest I felt positively Lilliputian. This enormous tree is named after a general who fought in the Civil War; it is nearly 300 ft. high, 112 ft. round and has a diameter of 41 ft. at its base. "General Sherman" is reckoned to be 3,500 years old – the latest estimate is actually 3,600. Its weight must be in the region of 7,000 tons. One thing is certain, that the eye is far more use than the camera here, since these giant trees stand not alone, but in groups.

Dort steigt der Libby Tree bis über 100 Meter hoch in den Himmel. Im Riesenwald (Giant Forest) kam ich mir vor wie ein Winzling gegenüber dem „General Sherman". Nach diesem Heerführer im amerikanischen Bürgerkrieg ist die gewaltige Sequoia genannt. Ihre Höhe beträgt 90 Meter, der Stammesumfang 34 Meter und sein Durchmesser an der Basis 12,5 Meter. Man schätzt das Alter des „General Sherman" auf 3500, neuerdings sogar auf 3600 Jahre. Das Gewicht des schwersten aller Waldkönige soll 7000 Tonnen betragen. Jedoch, das Auge sieht mehr, als die Kamera festhalten kann, denn die Giganten stehen in Gruppen beisammen. Also verdeckt einer den anderen.

Le Libby Tree atteint là jusqu'à 100 mètres de haut. Dans la Vallée des Géants (Giant Forest), je me suis senti minuscule face au «General Sherman». C'est d'après ce général engagé dans la guerre civile américaine qu'a été baptisé l'imposant Sequoia. Il a 90 mètres de haut; le tour de l'arbre ne fait pas moins de 34 mètres; le diamètre à la base mesure 12,5 mètres. Le plus lourd des rois de la forêt pèse dans les 7000 tonnes. L'œil perçoit toutefois davantage que la caméra; ici, un arbre en cache véritablement un autre.

pages 74/75: Sequoia "General Sherman"

National Parks
ANIMALS OF THE WILDERNESS

Chipmunks live in burrows and their diet consists of seeds, berries and nuts, although they are not averse to robbing nests if they have the chance. They are regarded as a delicacy by the grizzlies and other bears, who can dig a chipmunk out from three feet under the earth in minutes. Grizzly bears may not look especially fast movers, but it is surprising how rapidly they will go in chase of prey or climb a tree. The mule deer prefers a habitat of sparse conifer woods, although at night and also in areas where it can live undisturbed, it will often roam into open country or even into semi-desert.

Die Streifenhörnchen, in ihrem Verbreitungsgebiet Chipmunk genannt, wohnen in Erdbauten. Meist leben sie vegetarisch von Samen, Beeren und Nüssen, betreiben jedoch bei passender Gelegenheit Nesträuberei. Ihrerseits sind die Chipmunks bei den Grizzlies und anderen Bären beliebt. Auch wenn der Grizzly-Bär nicht nach einem flinken Renner aussieht, ist er doch sehr beweglich, jagt hinter Beute her und klettert Bäume hinauf. Der Maultierhirsch bevorzugt als Einstand lichte Nadelholzwälder. Aber bei Nacht, oder wenn die Gegend einigermaßen ungestört ist, zieht er auch weit in die Steppe.

Les écureuils rayés appelés Chipmunk dans leur région natale, vivent dans des constructions sous la terre. Ils sont en principe végétariens et se nourrissent de graines, de baies et de noisettes. Mais quand l'occasion se présente, ils n'hésitent pas à aller voler des œufs dans les nids. Par ailleurs, ils sont très appréciés des grizzlies et autres espèces d'ours. Le grizzli est très mobile malgré son apparence pataude. Il chasse lestement sa proie et grimpe aux arbres. Le cerf préfère les forêts de pins clairsemées. Mais quand la nuit tombe ou que l'atmosphère est relativement tranquille, il peut s'enfoncer loin dans la prairie, jusque dans le demi-désert.

pages 76/77: From left to right:
chipmunk, grizzly bear, mule deer

Inyo National Forest
METHUSELAH PARK

The oldest of all living things can be found in Shulman Grove (Methuselah Park). At first sight the bristlecone pines are disappointing, especially if one has previously visited the sequoias. Bristlecone pines only grow to a height of 30 ft., and here wind and storms have wrought havoc with their branches. Six of them are over 4,000 years old, three are over 4,300 years old, and the Methuselah pine is the oldest living thing on earth, with an age of 4,625 years. This is not guesswork, but ascertained by a ring count made on samples taken by inserting an extremely fine hollow needle into the trunk.

Die ältesten Lebewesen gibt es nur in Shulman Grove, auch Methusala Park genannt. Zunächst werden Sie enttäuscht sein vom Anblick der Pinus aristatus, besonders wenn Sie vorher beide Arten der Sequoia gesehen haben. Die Borstenzapfenkiefer wird nur wenige Meter hoch, all ihre Äste sind von Wind und Sturm zerzaust. Sechs Exemplare sind über 4000 Jahre alt, drei haben mehr als 4300 Jahre hinter sich, während der Methusalem mit 4625 Jahren als ältestes Lebewesen auf unserer Erde gelten darf. Gemessen hat man das Alter mit Hilfe einer fadendünnen Hohlnadel. Sie wird in die Bristleconepine gestochen, an der herausgeholten Substanz zählt man die Jahresringe.

Il faut en faire du chemin pour passer des êtres vivants les plus grands et les plus lourds de la terre aux plus anciens. Ils n'existent en effet qu'à un seul endroit des Etats-Unis, dans le Shulman Grove, également appelé Methusala Park. Le Pinus aristatus commencera sûrement par décevoir, surtout si l'on a pu admirer auparavant les deux sortes de Sequoia. Ces sortes de conifères, en effet, n'ont que quelques mètres de haut; leurs branches ont été dépouillées par le vent et les tempêtes. Six de ces arbres ont plus de 4000 ans, trois ont plus de 4300 ans; quant au Methusalem, il peut prétendre, avec ses 4625 ans, être l'être vivant le plus ancien de la terre.

pages 78/79: Inyo National Forest, bristlecone pines.

Death Valley
NATIONAL MONUMENT

Death Valley National Monument, in the east of the Sierra Nevada, is a must for tourists, although it should be warned that the temperature can reach over 120 Fahrenheit in summer. About five per cent of this huge area lies below sea level and in a hollow near Badwater there is the lowest place in the USA, at a depth of 282 ft. below sea level. Death Valley first became known when it was explored in the 1849 Gold Rush, for people assumed it to be the most direct route to California.

Unbedingt sehenswert ist das Todestal im Osten der Sierra Nevada, ein Nationalmonument des kalifornischen Staates, aber Vorsicht im Sommer, wenn die Temperatur auf 56° Celsius steigt. Etwa fünf Prozent des riesengroßen Gebietes liegen unter der Meereshöhe. Eine Mulde bei Badlands ist mit 86 Metern unter Null die allertiefste Stelle der USA. Erst 1849, als in Kalifornien der Goldrausch ausbrach und man glaubte, der schnellste Weg führe durch das Todestal, wurde die Gegend erkundet und bekannt.

Déclarée Monument National de l'Etat californien, la Vallée de la Mort est une curiosité qu'il faut absolument visiter. Mais attention: en été, la température peut grimper au-dessus de 50 degrés Celsius. Près de 5% de cet immense territoire est situé en-dessous du niveau de la mer. Le point le plus bas des Etats-Unis est une cuvette, près de Badlands: près de 90 mètres en-dessous du niveau de la mer. La Vallée de la Mort n'a été connue et prospectée qu'en 1849, au moment où s'est déclenchée la ruées vers l'or en Californie et où l'on croyait que le moyen le plus rapide d'y parvenir était de traverser cette région désertique.

pages 80/81: Badwater Pool (282 feet below sea level).
In the background is Telescope Peak (11,049 ft. high).

UTAH
Zion National Park

It is common knowledge that the state of Utah was founded by the Mormons, who still make up the majority of the population; less well-known is the fact that one of the most interesting natural phenomena in North America is to be found in the south of the state, in the ZION NATIONAL PARK. It is the Zion Canyon, a narrow, deep gorge which glows in all sorts of colours according to the angle of the sun. The main entrance is at the beginning of the canyon, where the Visitors' Center will provide all the required information.

Im Süden des Staates Utah, der bekanntlich von den Mormonen gegründet wurde, die auch heute noch die Mehrzahl der Bevölkerung stellen, gibt es eines der weniger bekannten, doch äußerst interessanten Naturwunder Nordamerikas, den über 1000 Quadratkilometer großen ZION-NATIONALPARK. Das erstaunlichste ist dort der Zion-Canyon, eine ebenso enge wie tiefe Schlucht, die je nach Sonneneinfall in verschiedenen Farben schimmert. Der Canyon beginnt gleich beim Haupteingang, wo man im Visitors Center alle Auskünfte erhält.

L'Etat d'Utah, fondé par les Mormons qui continuent aujourd'hui encore d'en constituer la majorité de la population, offre au sud l'une de ces merveilles de la nature d'Amérique du Nord qui, si elles sont moins connues, n'en restent pas moins extrêmement intéressantes: le PARC NATIONAL DE ZION, d'une superficie de 1000 kilomètres carrés. Le plus marquant, dans ce parc, est le canyon de Zion, une gorge aussi étroite que profonde qui prend les couleurs les plus diverses suivant la position du soleil. Le canyon commence dès l'entrée du parc où se trouve également un Visitors Center donnant toutes les informations nécessaires.

page 82: Zion National Park, Temple of Snawava

UTAH
Zion National Park

There are roughly 250 clearly-marked footpaths in this wild and rugged landscape, but roads are scarce. Kolob Canyon is even narrower and its almost vertical sides consist of red sandstone that glistens blood-red at sundown. Nearby there are the remarkable natural bridges and bizarre pock formations that have been given the names of exotic temples that they often resemble from afar.

Nur wenige Autowege führen durch das wildzerrissene Gelände, aber etwa 250 gut markierte Wanderwege. Im Kolob-Canyon, noch enger als die Zion-Schlucht, bestehen die fast senkrechten Wände aus rotem Sandstein, der bei sinkender Sonne blutrot leuchtet. Nicht weit davon entfernt bestaunt man die von der Natur geschaffenen Brücken und bizarren Felsformationen. Sie bekamen die Namen von exotischen Tempeln, weil man sie, aus der Ferne betrachtet, dafür halten kann.

Cette zone accidentée et sauvage n'est traversée que de quelques routes seulement; elle compte en revanche 250 chemins de randonnée bien marqués. Dans le Canyon de Kolob, plus étroit encore que la gorge de Zion, les parois rocheuses presque verticales sont d'un grès rouge qui devient rouge sang au coucher du soleil. Non loin de là, l'on peut admirer les ponts et les formations rocheuses bizarres que la nature a créés; ils ont été baptisés «temples exotiques»; c'est de fait l'impression qu'ils donnent, vus de loin.

page 84: Zion National Park, Mezozoic sandstone formation (136 million years old)
page 85: Zion National Park, The Three Patriarchs

UTAH
Bryce Canyon
NATIONAL PARK

Bryce Canyon National Park, with an area of 35 square miles, is another of the wonders of Utah. The American Automobile Club, the AAA, brashly describes it as having' the most colourful rocks on the face of the earth', which isn't far wrong. There is a natural amphitheatre whose horseshoe of rocks glows blood-red or golden yellow as the sun changes position, with deep brown rocks behind and lavender-coloured above.

Ebenfalls im Staat Utah erlebt man den Bryce-Canyon-Nationalpark mit 9000 Hektar. Keineswegs bescheiden erklärt das „Touring-Buch" des amerikanischen Automobilclubs (AAA), daß der Bryce-Park die „farbigsten Felsen der ganzen Erdkruste" enthält. Man könnte wirklich diesen Eindruck gewinnen. Denn es gibt dort von der Natur geschaffene Amphitheater, deren riesige Hufeisen blutrot leuchten oder goldengelb, je nach dem Sonnenstand. Tiefbraune Felsen sind gleich dahinter und lavendelfarbene darüber.

C'est également dans l'Etat d'Utah que se trouve le Parc National du Bryce-Canyon, d'une superficie de 9000 hectares. Le guide touristique de l'Automobile-Club américain (AAA) explique sans modestie aucune que le Parc du Bryce-Canyon renferme «les rochers les plus colorés de la croûte terrestre». C'est réellement l'impresion que l'on peut avoir : la nature a créé là un amphithéâtre de pierre, un immense fer à cheval, rouge sang ou jaune d'or suivant la position du soleil.

page 86: Bryce Canyon, natural bridge

UTAH
Bryce Canyon
NATIONAL PARK

The erosion over millions of years by wind, water and the swirling currents of the River Paria has created such colours and formations that from a distance one imagines one is seeing castles, towers and mediaeval fortresses, gothic churches with hundreds of sculptures. The outlines are weird and fantastic.

Die Erosion von Wind und Wasser, auch die Strudel des Paria-Flusses haben in Jahrmillionen die Farben und Formationen geschaffen. Von weitem glaubt man Burgen, Türme und mittelalterliche Schlösser zu sehen, auch hochgotische Kirchen mit vielen hundert Skulpturen. Sagenhaft unwirklich sind die Konturen. Näher hinein und höher hinauf führen gut begehbare Wege.

Un peu plus loin se dressent des rochers d'un brun profond suivis, un peu plus loin encore, de rochers couleur lavande. C'est le travail d'érosion effectué par les vents et les eaux ainsi que les tourbillons du fleuve Paria qui ont fait naître, au cours de plusieurs millions d'années, ces formations rocheuses et ces couleurs. De loin, l'on pense voir des châteaux-forts, des tours, des châteaux moyenâgeux, voire même des églises gothiques avec des centaines et des centaines de sculptures. Les contours paraissent merveilleusement irréels.

Bryce Canyon
NATIONAL PARK

Only when the visitor approaches on the well-trodden paths leading into and around the canyon does it become obvious that none of this is man-made; here the hand of the Creator has been at work. Along the Peek-a-boo Trail, gigantic natural windows pierce the towering cliff faces, while in Bridge Canyon there is an enormous cave and Tower Bridge, a rock formation resembling its namesake in London.

Erst aus relativ naher Entfernung begreift der Besucher, daß bei all dem keines Menschen Hand am Werke war, sondern allein die Naturkräfte des Schöpfers. Entlang dem Peek-a-boo Trail bestaunt der Wanderer in den himmelhohen Felsmauern eine Reihe von Riesenfenstern. Im Bridge-Canyon öffnet sich eine Riesenhöhle, und die Tower-Bridge (Turmbrücke) verbindet auf halber Höhe zwei Felsentürme miteinander.

Il est possible de s'approcher du canyon par des chemins praticables qui mènent également sur les hauteurs. Ce n'est qu'au dernier moment que le visiteur comprend qu'il ne s'agit pas d'une création de l'homme, mais le fruit du jeu des forces de la nature, l'œuvre du Créateur. Tout le long de la piste appelée Peek-a-boo Trail, le marcheur restera muet d'admiration devant d'immenses fenêtres taillées dans la roche. Dans le Bridge-Canyon s'ouvre une immense caverne et la Pont de la Tour (Tower-Bridge) relie à mi-hauteur deux tours de pierre entre elles.

Bryce Canyon
AMPHITHEATER

Pumas, mule deer, grey foxes, marmots, prairie dogs, squirrels and a diversity of multicoloured birds are to found in Bryce Canyon. Up to the twelfth century, the narrow valleys were populated by the Paiute, a relatively civilised Indian tribe of which there are still some survivors in the reservations. Bryce Canyon is open all the year round, although the roads are often blocked during a hard winter.

Berglöwen, Maultierhirsche, Graufüchse und Murmeltiere, auch Präriehunde, Eichhörnchen und eine Vielfalt bunter Vögel beleben den Bryce-Nationalpark. Menschen dagegen sind selten, und sie waren es schon in alter Zeit. Die Anasazi, was weiter nichts bedeutet als „die Alten", haben bis zum zwölften Jahrhundert die engen Täler bewohnt. Die Payuten, ein relativ hochentwickelter Indianerstamm, von denen heute noch Reste in Reservaten leben, sind ihnen gefolgt. Der Bryce-Canyon ist während des ganzen Jahres für Besucher geöffnet, nur in strengen Wintern müssen die Straßen gesperrt werden.

Pumas, chevreuils américains (Muledeers), renards gris, marmottes, chiens des prairies, écureuils et une quantité d'oiseaux bigarrés animent le Parc National de Bryce. Les hommes, par contre, sont rares. Les Anasazi (ce qui signifie les «Anciens») ont habité les vertes vallées jusqu'au 12ème siècle. Les Paiutes, une tribu d'Indiens considérée, toute proportion gardée, comme hautement évoluée et qui existe encore dans quelques réserves, ont pris la relève. Le Bryce-Canyon est ouvert toute l'année au visiteur; il n'y a que pendant les rudes hivers que les routes sont fermées.

Canyonlands/Arches
NATIONAL PARK

In the south-west of Utah, at the confluence of the Colorado and the Green River, there is to be found the very latest national park, Canyonlands, an area of over 40 sq. miles. A lot of its roads are scarcely past the planning stage, with the advantage that the park is still in its original state and not overrun by tourists. Broad, open plateaus alternate with deep river valleys, high domes of rock and steep cliffs. Human hands have had no part to play in this landscape, which has remained unchanged for thousands of years. It is impossible to visit all the sights of Canyonlands, but on no account to be missed is Arches Monument, a specially designated area that contains 89 natural bridges.

Der neueste Nationalpark im Südosten des Staates Utah ist Canyonland (10 500 Hektar), gelegen am Zusammenfluß des Colorado mit dem Green River. Viele der geplanten Straßen sind vorerst nicht fertig. Weite freie Flächen wechseln ab mit tiefen Flußtälern, mit Felsendomen und steilen Wänden. Der Mensch hat in dieser Gegend nicht eingegriffen, die ganze Region ist geblieben, wie sie vor vielen Tausend Jahren gewesen ist. Alles kann man nicht sehen im Canyonland, aber Arches Monument, ein für 89 Naturbrücken bestimmtes Schutzgebiet, soll man unter keinen Umständen auslassen.

Le dernier Parc National aménagé dans le Sud-Est de l'Etat d'Utah est celui du Canyon (10 500 hectares), situé au confluent du Colorado et de la Green River. D'immenses espaces libres alternent avec des vallées profondes, des dômes de pierre et des parois abruptes. Cette région est vestée intacte; elle n'a pas changé depuis des milliers d'années. Il est impossible de tout voir dans ce Parc National, mais il est une chose qu'il faut admirer à tout prix: l'Arches Monument, une zone comptant 89 ponts naturels crées de toute pièce par la nature elle-même.

Canyonlands/Arches
THE WINDOWS

The landscape is stony, sandy, with thorn bushes, and in colours beyond the traveller's wildest dreams. The high bridges that span the great river valleys are the products of erosion by wind and water; some even appear filigree in texture. Few of these incredible formations are accessible by road; the rest can only be seen on foot, and anyone who wants to visit, or dares to cross, the more remote ones has to be an experienced climber. It would be impossible to visit all 89 bridges, but three or four are quite enough.

Dort erlebt der Besucher eine Landschaft aus Fels, Sand und Dornbüschen in Farben, die phantastischer sind als jede Vorstellung. Felsbrücken überspannen weit und hoch die ausgewaschenen Flußtäler. Manche der Brücken, von Wind, Wasser und Erosion geschaffen, erscheinen dem Menschenauge als feines Filigran. Nur an wenige der sagenhaften Gebilde kann der Besucher auf guten Straßen heranfahren, meist kommt man nur zu Fuß in die Nähe. Wer auch die selten besuchten Naturwunder sehen will, womöglich gar den Übergang wagen möchte, muß an Klettern gewöhnt sein. Alle 89 Brücken zu betrachten, dürfte unmöglich sein, drei oder vier genügen ja auch.

Il s'offre ici au visiteur un paysage de roches, de sable et d'arbustes épineux dans des couleurs fantastiques dépassant l'imagination. Des ponts de pierre surplombent les belles vallées fluviales. Certains d'entre eux, œuvres du vent, de l'eau et de l'érosion, sont perçus comme de fins ouvrages de filigrane. Quelques-unes seulement de ces formations extraordinaires sont accessibles par la route. La plupart du temps, on ne peut s'en approcher qu'à pied. Celui qui veut admirer ces merveilles de la nature ou même se risquer à les franchir, doit être habitué à l'escalade. Il est impossible de voir tous les 89 ponts, trois ou quatre suffisent d'ailleurs.

Canyonlands

Mysterious cave drawings, or petroglyphs, in the Painted Desert in Arizona. They are said to date from the thirteenth century and their white discoverers gave them the name "Newspaper Rock" in the belief that they were some sort of tribal newssheet for the Indians. The current theory is that they represent magic hunting spells etched into the stone to favour the capture of certain desirable animals. The human hand seems to indicate seizure of property.

Rätselhafte Steinzeichnungen – Petroglyphen – in der „Painted Desert" in Arizona. Sie sollen aus dem 13. Jahrhundert stammen, und „Newspaper-Rock" (Zeitungsfelsen) wird das Gebilde genannt, weil die weißen Entdecker glaubten, es handelte sich um Schriftbildberichte eines indianischen Volkes. Heute aber ist man eher der Meinung, es sei Jagdzauber, der in Stein gekratzte Wunsch, bestimmte Tiere zu erbeuten. Dabei gilt vermutlich die Menschenhand als Zeichen der Besitzergreifung.

De mystérieux dessins rupestres – des pétroglyphes – dans le «Painted Desert» de l'Arizona. Ils proviendraient du treizième siècle et sont appelés «Newspaper-Rock» (journal dans la roche) car les découvreurs croyaient qu'il s'agissait des rapports écrits d'un peuple indien. On pense aujourd'hui qu'ils représentent des signes de magie indigène. L'espoir, gravé dans la pierre, de capturer certaines proies. La main humaine symboliserait la prise de possession.

page 102: Arches National Park, showing the author Hans-Otto Meissner on one of the natural bridges.
page 103: Indian Petroglyphen

Mesa Verde

INDIAN CLIFF DWELLINGS

800 years ago, the Anasazi built cliff dwellings inside deep and often damp cave. These cave houses – one is almost tempted to say towns – sometimes have over one hundred rooms, and a few have as many as one hundred and thirty five. In about the year 1400 all the caves were abandoned, presumably because of recurring droughts. There are many different kinds of cliff dwellings in the Mesas, most of them in the large Navajo reservation.

In den tiefen, oft feuchten Höhlen haben sich die „Anasazi" ihre Höhlenhäuser, fast könnte man sagen ihre Höhlenstädte gebaut. Manche enthalten mehr als 100, sogar bis 135 Räume. Um das Jahr 1400 wurden alle Höhlen verlassen, vermutlich weil zu große Trockenheit über das Land kam. Es gibt viele, sehr verschiedenartige Cliff Dwellings in den Mesas, fast alle befinden sich im großen Reservat der Navajo-Indianer.

C'est dans ces cavernes profondes, souvent humides que les «Anasazi» ont construit des demeures, voire même des villes souterraines. Certaines cavernes en effet comprennent plus de cent salles, d'autres en abritent plus de cent-trente-cinq. Vers 1400, toutes ces cavernes furent abandonnées, sans doute à la suite d'une grande sécheresse qui s'était abattue sur le pays. Les mesas comprennent une grande variété de Cliff Dwellings. Presque toutes se trouvent dans la grande réserve des Indiens Navajos.

page 104: Cliff Palace
page 105: Tower House

Indian Pow Wow

Every year members of many of the Indian tribes gather in Arizona and New Mexico for the Great Pow-wow, which keeps alive the ancient customs in ceremonial dances, songs and contests.

The bison used to provide the Indians with all the basic necessities of life, although there were 60 million bison and the Indians never posed any threat to the survival of the species. That came 150 years ago when the white settlers arrived with their firearms and slaughtered so many bison that at one point only 350 animals remained. Subsequent protective measures have meant that their numbers have increased to roughly 30,000.

Alljährlich treffen sich in Arizona und New Mexico Mitglieder vieler Indianerstämme zu ihrem großen Pow Wow, zur Pflege alter zeremonieller Tänze, Gesänge und Wettkämpfe.

Das Bison war in früheren Zeiten die Lebensgrundlage der Indianer, die den Tierbestand von ursprünglich 60 Millionen Tieren nicht bedrohten. Erst die weißen Einwanderer hatten vor 150 Jahren den Bestand auf 850 Exemplare durch Abschüsse mit Feuerwaffen dezimiert. Die späteren Schutzmaßnahmen haben den Bestand wieder auf annähernd 30 000 Tiere anwachsen lassen.

Chaque année, les membres de nombreuses tribus indiennes se rencontrent en Arizona et au Nouveau Mexique. Au cours d'une grande célébration appelée «Pow Wow», ils pratiquent les chants, danses et luttes traditionelles.

Autrefois, le bison formait la nourriture de base des Indiens sans que le troupeau de 60 millions de bêtes à l'origine en soit menacé pour autant. Mais quand les pionniers arrivèrent, il y a 150 ans, ils utilisèrent des armes à feu et réduisirent le cheptel à 850 bêtes. Grâce aux mesures de protection prises ultérieurement, le troupeau comprend aujourd'hui près de 30 000 bêtes.

page 106:   BISON. This photo was voted best bison
                picture in an international competition.
pages 108/109: Monument Valley, "The Mittens"

ARIZONA
Monument Valley
THE MITTENS

Monument Valley is another extensive region belonging to the increasing numbers of Navajo Indians. John Newbury, the first white geologist to explore the area, wrote of his journey in 1854 that for seven days he had wandered through the city of the Cyclops. Monument Valley does indeed resemble the deserted and ruined town of a race of giant beings, a shimmering rose-pink scene of devastation.

Auch das Monument-Valley, das „Tal der Denkmäler", gehört zum weiten Stammesgebiet der sich rasch vermehrenden Navajo-Indianer. Er sei sieben Tage lang durch eine Zyklopenstadt gewandert, hat John Newbury berichtet, der 1854 als erster weißer Geologe die Gegend erkundet hat. Wie Ruinen der Riesen, wie die verlassene Stadt eines Gigantenvolkes sieht Monument-Valley aus. Das Ganze ist ein rosarot schimmerndes Trümmerfeld.

La «Monument-Valley», la Vallée des Monuments, fait partie du vaste territoire des Navajos, un peuple indien en plein essor. John Newbury, le premier géologue blanc à avoir exploré la région en 1854, rapporte qu'il marcha durant sept jours à travers une ville de cyclopes. La Monument Valley ressemble en effet à une ville de géants abandonnée et en ruines. L'ensemble fait penser à un champ de décombres rougeâtres.

pages 110/111: Monument Valley, "The Mittens"

Arizona

On all sides, haunted castles and antediluvian skyscrapers, stupendous arches, circular sandstone plinths and monumental pillars combine to create utterly indescribable scenery. There are only twenty Navajo families as permanent residents. Their sheep graze the barren land and the wool is woven into the famous Navajo rugs by the industrious women of the tribe. Some families still live in the ancient huts named hogans. Anyone who has the luck to be here in pouring rain has the chance of photographing the reflection of the stone towers in the pools.

Geisterburgen und vorsintflutliche Wolkenkratzer, gewaltige Bögen, kreisrunde Sandsteinsokkel und himmelhohe Säulen bilden nach allen Seiten eine so phantastische Kulisse, daß sie mit Worten nicht zu beschreiben ist. Nur zwanzig Navajo-Familien sind ständige Bewohner. Deren Schafe weiden auf dem wenig fruchtbaren Boden, und aus ihrer Wolle weben fleißige Frauen die weithin berühmten Navajo-Decken. Einige Familien leben heute noch in den „Hogan" genannten Hütten der alten Zeit. Wer großes Glück hat und strömenden Regen erlebt, kann im stehenden Wasser das Spiegelbild der Steintürme fotografieren.

Châteaux hantés et gratte-ciel antédiluviens, arcs imposants, socles de grès ronds et colonnes géantes forment un décor si fantastique que les mots ne sont pas assez forts pour le décrire. Vingt familles de Navajos seulement y demeurent en permanence. Les moutons qu'elles font paître sur les sols arides donnent la laine que les Indiennes tissent inlassablement pour produire les célèbres couvertures navajos. Quelques familles vivent encore dans les huttes anciennes appelées «hogan». Celui qui a la chance de vivre une pluie diluvienne peut photographier le reflet des tours de pierre dans les eaux stagnantes.

page 112: Monument Valley/"The Totem Pole",
Yei-bi-chei-group
page 113: Canyon de Chelly, Spider Rock

ARIZONA
Canyon de Chelly

I've been to the Canyon de Chelly three times altogether and I'm already looking forward to a fourth visit. In my opinion it has no equal in the Southwest of the USA, having so much to offer in the way of attractive landscape and historical remains, along with its water, rocks, people and animals. The narrow ravine, nearly thirty-five miles long, with smooth, steep sides nearly one thousand feet high, is to be found in Navajo territory, as indeed are so many other famous sights of the area.

Im Canyon de Chelly bin ich dreimal gewesen und freue mich schon jetzt auf das vierte Mal. So viel an landschaftlichem Reiz, an geschichtlichen Relikten, auch an Wasser, Fels, Menschen und Tieren kommt dort zusammen, daß es meines Erachtens im Südwesten der USA nichts besseres gibt. Wie so manche der großen Sehenswürdigkeiten gehört die 56 Kilometer lange Schlucht mit ihren 300 Meter hohen, glatten Seitenwänden zum Stammesgebiet, besser gesagt zum Staatsgebiet der Navajos.

J'ai déjà visité trois fois le Canyon de Chelly et me réjouis fort à l'idée de m'y rendre une quatrième fois. Le paysage est d'un charme tel, il existe une si grande quantité de survivances historiques, une telle diversité, qu'il s'agisse d'eaux, de roches, d'hommes ou d'animaux, qu'à mon avis, le Sud-Ouest des Etats-Unis n'a vien de plus enchanteur à offrir. Tout comme un certain nombre des plus grandes curiosités, cette longue gorge de 56 kilomètres de long, délimitée par des parois lisses de 300 mètres de haut, appartient à la réserve, disons plutôt au territoire national des Navajos.

ARIZONA
Indian Cliff Dwellings

In spring the rushing melt-water of the rivers sees the returns of roughly three hundred Navajos, accompanied by their wives, children, sheep and horses, to the canyon which has been the summer home of this particular clan for around five hundred years. The Anasazi also converted a few cliff caves into veritable castles. The White House is an especially interesting example, if one is prepared to climb the steep, narrow steps cut into the rock to see it. Several of the caves have artistic wall paintings, while in others well-preserved mummies have been found.

Wenn im Frühjahr das rauschende Schmelzwasser abläuft, kehren rund 300 Navajos mit Frauen und Kindern, mit ihren Schafen und Pferden ins Canyon zurück. Es ist für die Mitglieder eines bestimmten Clans seit etwa fünf Jahrhunderten die Sommerheimat. Auch hier haben sich die Anasazi ein paar der Seitenhöhlen zu Wohnburgen ausgebaut. Besonders interessant das „Weiße Haus", aber nur zugänglich über in Fels gehauene schmale und steile Stufen. Manche der Höhlen sind kunstvoll ausgemalt, in anderen hat man gut erhaltene Mumien gefunden.

Au printemps, à la fonte des neiges, quelque 300 Navajos réintègrent le canyon avec femmes, enfants, chevaux et moutons. Depuis près de cinq siècles, le canyon est la résidence d'été d'un des clans. Ici aussi, les Anasazis ont transformé quelques cavernes latérales en maisons d'habitation. Il en existe une, particulièrement intéressante, la «maison blanche» accessible seulement par des marches étroites et abruptes taillées dans la pierre. Certaines cavernes sont décorées de belles peintures murales, dans d'autres, l'on a découvert des momies bien conservées.

page 118: White House Ruin, Canyon de Chelly, Arizona
page 119: Betatakin ruin, Indian cliff dwelling, 13th c.

Glen Canyon
LAKE POWELL

In the south-east of Utah, on the upper reaches of the Colorado River, we can see the hand of man at work, and what's more, in the grand style. There are gigantic dams along the Colorado, although they have by no means destroyed the landscape; quite the reverse, in fact, for there has been created a chain of emerald-green lakes, each one more beautiful than the next, to prove that hydraulic power stations need not only be an economic necessity, but can also make a positive contribution to the landscape. Lake Powell reflects the surrounding rocks that are white to light grey above, pink shading into deep red below.

Im Südosten von Utah, am Oberlauf des Colorado-River, waren Menschen am Werk, sogar im großen Stil. Sie haben den Colorado gestaut und mit gewaltigen Dämmen versehen. Aber die Natur haben sie nicht verschandelt, ganz im Gegenteil. Eine Kette von Seen ist entstanden, einer schöner als der andere und smaragdgrün jeder. Ein Beweis, daß Wasserkraftwerke nicht nur einen wirtschaftlichen, sondern auch landschaftlichen Segen bedeuten können. Helles bis grauweißes, in tiefen Lagen rosarotes bis tiefrotes Gestein umgibt den Lake Powell und spiegelt sich darin.

L'homme a créé une œuvre colossale dans le Sud-Est de l'Utah, sur le cours supérieur de la Colorado-River. Il a endigué le Colorado et l'a pourvu de barrages gigantesques sans pour autant détruire la nature. Bien au contraire. On peut aujourd'hui admirer une chaîne de lacs de couleur émeraude, tous plus enchanteurs les uns que les autres. Une preuve que des centrales hydro-électriques ne constituent pas seulement un bienfait pour l'économie, mais aussi quelquefois pour le paysage. Des roches du blanc au gris clair, du rose au pourpre dans leurs couches inférieures entourent le pac Powel et se reflètent dans ses eaux.

Utah/Arizona

Erosion has created here as elsewhere natural bridges, knights' castles, church steeples and ancient temples. Incidentally, John Powell, after whom the great tourist attraction of Lake Powell is named, was a real daredevil. He shot the rapids of the Colorado for a good sixty miles in 1867, a trip which took him through the narrowest and deepest stretches of the Grand Canyon. He was the first to perform this feat, although nowadays whole groups of tourists can have the journey organized for them.

Auch dort Naturbrücken, Ritterburgen, Kirchtürme und antike Tempel, allesamt durch Erosion entstanden. Im übrigen war John Powell, auf dessen Namen der vielbesuchte See getauft ist, ein tollkühner Bursche. Er schoß im Jahr 1867 auf wildschäumenden Wellen einhundert Kilometer weit den Colorado-River herunter. Dabei durchfuhr der kühne Mann auch die schmalste und tiefste Stelle des Grand Canyon. Niemand hatte es vor ihm gewagt, aber heute wird das für Touristengruppen organisiert.

Là aussi, l'érosion a créé des ponts naturels, des forts, des tours d'églises et des temples antiques. Le lac qui reçoit de nombreux visiteurs porte le nom d'un homme téméraire. En 1867, Georges Powell défia sur cent kilomètres en aval les eaux tourmentées de la Colorado-River. L'audacieux traversa les endroits les plus étroits et profonds du Grand Canyon. Avant lui, personne n'avait osé cette entreprise périlleuse qui aujourd'hui est organisée pour des groupes de touristes.

page 122: UTAH/Lake Powell, Rainbow Bridge
page 123: Arizona/Petrified Forest

Petrified Forest

In the centre of Arizona's Painted Desert lies the Petrified Forest. 200 million years ago this region turned to marshland; aging trees could no longer keep upright and fell into the swamp. Water rich in silicon was absorbed by the cells, releasing silicic acid and creating rock crystal, agate, amethyst and carnelian. The shape and cell structure of the tree trunks remained unchanged.

In der bunten Wüste von Arizona, inmitten des Painted Desert, liegt der „versteinerte Wald" – der Petrified Forest. Vor 200 Millionen Jahren dehnte sich hier ein weites Sumpfgebiet aus, so daß die alten Bäume umstürzten und ins Moor fielen. In ihre Zellen drang das siliziumhaltige Wasser ein, hinterließ Kieselsäure und kristallisierte zu Bergkristall, Achat, Amethyst und Karneol. Die Form und Zellstruktur der Baumstämme blieb hierbei erhalten.

La «forêt pétrifiée» – la Petrified Forest s'étend au milieu du Painted Desert, le désert peint de l'Arizona. Un vaste marécage recouvrait la région il y a 200 millions d'années. Quand les arbres atteignaient un certain âge, ils s'écroulaient et s'enfonçaient dans les marais. L'eau riche en silicium pénétrait dans leurs cellules, y déposait du silicate et se cristallisait pour former du cristal de roche, de l'agate, de l'améthyste et de la cornaline. La forme et la structure des troncs d'arbres restèrent conservées.

page 125: The Kalanchoe is a water-retaining species of succulent. It is only an inch or two high and can be found in the Petrified Forest in Arizona's Painted Desert.

Arizona
SEDONA

Sedona, a town much frequented by tourists and retired folk, enjoys an exceptionally attractive and open position, with a background of shimmering pinkish sandstone hills. The surrounding protected area offers a number of routes leading directly to the romantic seclusion of the wilderness named Oak Creek Canyon. The rock formations here are amazing; seen from afar, the crag in this picture could easily be mistaken for a cathedral.

Sedona, ebenso beliebt bei Touristen wie Pensionisten, erfreut sich einer besonders schönen und freien Lage vor dem Hintergrund hellrot leuchtender Sandsteinberge. Von hier aus, wo die natürliche Umgebung besonderen Schutz genießt, führen die Wege schon bald in die romantische, im ungestörten Zustand belassene Wildnis des Oak Creek Canyons. Überaus eindrucksvoll erlebt man dort die Formationen der Gebirge. Von weitem könnte man das nebenstehende Felsgebilde für eine Kathedrale halten.

Sedona, aussi appréciée des touristes que des retraités, jouit d'une très belle situation. La ville s'étend devant un paysage de montagnes de grès aux lueurs rougeâtres. A partir de cet endroit, où la nature est spécialement protégée, les chemins conduisent très vite dans le site romantique et laissé à l'état sauvage du Canyon d'Oak Creek. Les formes des montagnes s'élèvent, impressionnantes, dans le ciel. De loin, l'œil pourrait prendre pour une cathédrale le tableau de roches qui se dresse devant nous.

ARIZONA
Grand Canyon
COLORADO RIVER

A visit to the Grand Canyon is a sufficient reason in itself for visiting America. The ravine and its surroundings have been a national park since 1909, and it is satisfying to note that further extensions are under way. In a few years' time it will be one link in a chain of such parks which will run from the north coast of California through Arizona and far into Utah. About one hundred and ten miles of the Colorado River belong to the national park. The canyon itself has a width of between 4,5 and 18 miles, and reaches a maximum depth of over 5,700 ft.

Der Grand Canyon des Colorado ist allein schon Grund genug, um nach Amerika zu fahren. Seit 1909 ist die Schlucht mit weiter Umgebung ein Nationalpark der USA, und erfreulicherweise wird das Schutzgebiet noch weiter ausgebaut. Mit all seinen benachbarten Parks wird es binnen weniger Jahre von der Nordküste Kaliforniens durch Arizona bis weit nach Utah reichen. Etwa 175 Kilometer des Colorado River gehören dazu. Der Canyon ist zwischen 7 und 29 Kilometer breit und an seiner tiefsten Stelle reicht es 1750 Meter hinab.

Le Grand Canyon du Colorado représente déjà une raison suffisante pour entreprendre un voyage aux Etats-Unis. Depuis 1909, la gorge et ses environs sont classés Parc national. Et on constate avec satisfaction que cette zone protégée ne cesse de s'élargir. Avec tous les parcs avoisinants, elle s'étendra d'ici quelques années de la côte nord californienne à travers l'Arizona jusqu'a l'Utah. 175 kilomètres de la Colorado-River en font partie. Le canyon large de sept à vingt-neuf kilomètres, tombe jusqu'à 1750 en ses plus profonds endroits.

pages 132/133: View from Hopi Point, high above the South Rim of the Grand Canyon; in the background Wotan's Throne, on the North Rim.

ARIZONA
Grand Canyon

The tourist centre of Grand Canyon Village, a town south of the river, caters for one and a half million visitors a year and provides all the necessities for mass tourism, although some people might find it enough just to watch sunrise and sunset from one of the vistapoints to the south. The changing light produces a kaleidoscope of magical effects. Even in winter, perhaps then more than ever, the snow-covered cliffs present a scene of fantastic beauty. The Grand Canyon is the longest and deepest ravine in the world.

Das Zentrum für Besucher, ungefähr 1,5 Millionen pro Jahr, ist die Ortschaft Grand Canyon Village auf der Südseite. Dort ist alles und jedes zu haben, was der Massentourismus braucht. Sonst aber genügt es, den Sonnenaufgang und den Untergang an einem Vistapoint der Südseite zu erleben. Ein Wunder des Lichts ist die alle paar Minuten wechselnde Beleuchtung. Sogar im Winter, erst recht im Winter, bieten die von Schnee bedeckten Hänge ein hinreißend schönes Schauspiel. Der Grand Canyon ist die längste und tiefste Schlucht der Welt.

Le Village du Grand Canyon attire le maximum de visiteurs, quelque 1,5 millions par an. Le tourisme de masse y trouve tout ce qu'il pourrait désirer. Mais aller admirer le lever ou le coucher du soleil d'un des points de vues du côté sud est déjà une expérience unique en son genre. Les jeux de lumière changeants à intervalles rapides sont un festin pour les yeux. En hiver surtout, les versants enneigés offrent un spectacle d'une beauté inouïe. Le Grand Canyon est la gorge la plus longue et la plus profonde du monde entier.

page 135: PUMA (Felis concolor)

Grand Canyon

A visit to the Havasu Ravine, a tributary valley of the Grand Canyon, offers a striking contrast, for this valley, in part over 5,250 ft. deep, is thickly wooded below and is inhabited by between 150 and 200 Indians of the Havasupai tribe (the word means green water people). The valley is an Indian reservation and the chief takes the decision whether to allow visitors into the territory. Those so privileged will be amazed at the fairytale landscape to be found in this relatively confined area.

Etwas völlig anderes bedeutet ein Besuch in der Havasu-Schlucht, einem Seitental des Grand Canyon. Das mehr als 1600 Meter tiefe Tal ist drunten dicht bewachsen und wird von 150 bis 200 Menschen bewohnt. Es sind die Havasupai, auf deutsch die Grünwassermenschen. Das Tal ist indianisches Reservat. Allein den Havasupai gehört es, und von ihrem Häuptling hängt ab, ob der Fremde hinunter darf. Wenn man es ihm gestattet, wird der Gast begeistert sein von der märchenhaften Landschaft auf relativ engem Raum.

La gorge de Havasu, voisine du Grand Canyon, présente une image tout à fait différente. Une végétation dense recouvre la vallée qui s'étend au fond du ravin profond de plus de 1600 mètres. De 150 à 200 personnes, les Havasupais ou hommes de l'eau verte, y ont établi leur demeure. Cette vallée, relativement étroite, leur appartient. C'est une réserve indienne. Un étranger ne peut y pénêtrer sans l'autorisation du chef de la tribu. Celui qui a la chance de la visiter sera émerveillé par le paysage de conte de fée qu'on découvre à chaque pas.

page 136:   Grand Canyon; aerial photograph of Havasu Canyon and Mooney Falls, with Havasu Falls in the background.
page 137:   Havasu Falls, Grand Canyon.
pages 138/139: Havasu Falls, Grand Canyon; a turquoise cascade of water flows from turbulent pools over ledges of travertine rock.

CALIFORNIA
Mojave Desert

Mojave is the Indian name for the desert and semi-desert of southern California. This hinterland of Los Angeles and San Diego is sparsely populated and possesses its own charm, especially in spring when the few plants are in full bloom. The JOSHUA TREE NATIONAL MONUMENT is well worth a visit; its name comes from the up to 40 ft. high Joshua trees. Their greenish-white flowers appear between March and May and can reach a size of 18 inches. In spring the Mojave is covered far and wide by the golden yellow branches, as thick as a finger, of the Octilla tree, and also by the low-growing flowering cactuses.

Mojave ist der indianische Name (gesprochen Mohjahvieh) für die Wüste und Halbwüste im südlichen Kalifornien, das heißt im Hinterland von Los Angeles und San Diego. Auch diese menschenarme Region hat ihren Reiz, besonders im Frühjahr, wenn der an sich sparsame Pflanzenwuchs in voller Blüte steht. Besonders lohnt sich der Besuch im JOSHUA-TREE-NATIO-NAL-MONUMENT, so genannt wegen der über 12 Meter hohen Joshuah-Bäume. Die grünweißen Blüten (von März bis Mai) erreichen eine Größe bis zu 45 Zentimeter. Weithin bedeckt ist die Mojave im Frühjahr auch von den goldgelben, fingerdicken Ästen des Ocotilla Baumes und den dicht am Boden blühenden Kakteen.

Mohave est le nom indien pour désigner les régions désertiques et semi-désertiques du Sud de la Californie, c'est à dire l'hinterland de Los Angeles et San Diego. Cette région dépeuplée possède également son charme, surtout au printemps lorsque la végétation rare fleurit. Vivement recommandée est la visite au JOSHUA-TREE-NATIONAL MONUMENT qui doit son nom aux arbres de Josuée dont la hauteur dépasse 12 mètres. Les fleurs blanches verdâtres de cet arbre s'épanouissent de mars à mai et atteignent jusqu'à 45 centimètres de diamètre. Des cactées en fleurs au raz du sol, les branches dorées de l'épaisseur d'un doigt de l'arbre ocotilla parsèment également le désert de Mohave durant la saison du printemps.

CALIFORNIA
San Diego

125 miles south of Los Angeles and only 16 miles from the Mexican border lies San Diego, the second largest city in California. It is a turbulent metropolis with superb parks, extensive beaches and sailing boats galore. The neighbouring campus of the University of California is also worth a visit. San Diego was used as a base for the Spanish settlement of California over the years, and the friary of San Diego Alcalá, founded in 1769, was the first of the chain of 21 missions of the Camino Real.
With this, we have returned to our point of departure, San Diego and the Camino Real, and thus our round trip of the south-west of the USA comes to an end.

San Diego ist die zweitgrößte Stadt Kaliforniens, 125 Meilen südlich von Los Angeles gelegen und nur 16 Meilen von der mexikanischen Grenze entfernt, eine turbulente Großstadt mit wundervollen Parks, weitläufigen Stränden und vielen Segelbooten in der Mission-Bucht. San Diego war zur spanischen Zeit die Basis für die allmähliche Erschließung des gesamten Kalifornien. Im Jahre 1769 wurde die Klostersiedlung von San Diego Alcalà gegründet und damit war sie die erste der 21 Missionen des „Camino Real".
Die Rundreise dieses Buches durch den Südwesten der USA hat in San Diego mit dem Camino Real begonnen und hier geht sie zu Ende.

San Diego est la deuxième ville de la Californie. Elle est située à 125 miles de Los Angeles et n'est éloignée que de 16 miles de la frontière mexicaine. San Diego est une grande ville turbulente, avec des parcs merveilleux, des plages à perte de vue et une armada de voiliers. Durant l'époque espagnole, c'est à San Diego que débuta l'exploitation progressive de toute la Californie. La communauté religieuse de San Diego Alcalà fut fondée en 1769.
Le circuit à travers le sud-ouest des Etats-Unis offert par cet ouvrage, a commencé au Camino Real et se termine ici, à San Diego.

page 142: Yucca Brevifolia, Joshua Tree Ntl. Monument